50 Chairs:
Innovations in Design and Materia

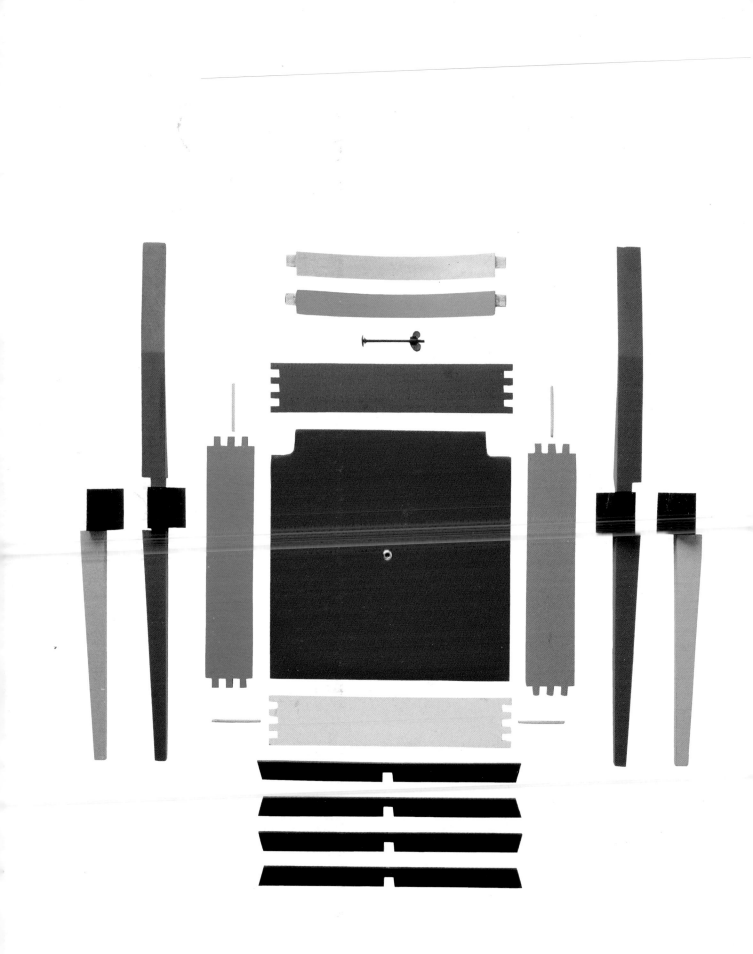

50 CHAIRS

Innovations in Design and Materials

Mel Byars

Introduction by
Alexander von Vegesack

Research by
Milena Brambilla
Cinzia Anguissola d'Altoé
Sara Puig

Technical drawings by
Thomas Tamburin

PRO DESIGN SERIES

▼RotoVision

▼RotoVision

Published by RotoVision SA
Rue du Rugnon, 7
1299 Crans-Prés-Celigny
Switzerland

RotoVision SA
Sales & Production Office
Sheridan House
112/116A Western Road
Hove BN3 IDD, England
Tel: 44-1273-7272-68
Fax: 44-1273-7272-69

Distributed to the trade in the United States
Watson-Guptill Publications
1515 Broadway
New York, NY 10036
U.S.A.

ISBN 2-88046-264-9

This book was written, designed, and
produced by Mel Byars.

Printed in Singapore
Production and separation
by ProVision Pte Ltd, Singapore
Tel: +65 334 7720
Fax: +65 334 7721

PRO DESIGN SERIES

50 Chairs: Innovations in Design and Materials
by Mel Byars with an Introduction by Alexander von Vegesack

50 Tables: Innovations in Design and Materials
by Mel Byars with an Introduction by Sylvain Dubuisson

50 Lights: Innovations in Design and Materials
by Mel Byars with an Introduction by Paola Antonelli

Contents

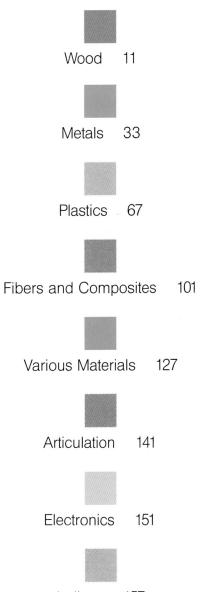

Introduction

While the basic function of chairs remains constant, technical developments have created an incredible variety of new possibilities for change in the construction and design of this furniture. Thus, seen throughout history, chairs offer a shimmering, revealing image of society, including the anachronisms for which they were created.

Chairs are objects with a soul, not only because they correspond to our physiology with their legs, seats, and backs or because they nurture us with their form and comfort but also because they possess an inner, well-conceived technology. However, we rarely recognize the fact that this technical construction is also a component conspicuously related to the design itself.

Mel Byars concentrates on the material and constructional aspect of chairs. But, while his approach is a technical one, his choices belie curiosity and subjectivity and are thus well suited to achieving his goal of reaching a broad audience. The spate of richly illustrated coffee table books that define today's generally superficial understanding of design identifies the quality of design only with the outer form and usually casts a blind eye to the technical achievements that characterize the form.

Here Byars sheds light on the incredible breadth of technological and thus often aesthetic innovations in furniture design. Hence, his book takes its place in what is an unfortunately all too rarely cultivated tradition of publications that create a broader understanding of furniture construction: Gustav Haßenpflug's *Stahlmöbel*, Karl Nothelfer's *Möbel*, Gerd Hatje's *New Furniture* series, and Mario Dal Fabbro's *Modern Furniture* defined the technical aspects of furniture design as early as the 1950s and '60s and served as eloquent testimonies to the Modern Movement. They explored a range of technology from the Windsor chair in turned and bent wood and Thonet's chairs in bent wood to furniture in tin and armchairs in tubing, whether hollow bamboo from the Philippines or extruded steel from Mannesmann.

A pioneering effort in this publishing tradition is Heinz and Bado Rasch's book, *Der Stuhl*, published in 1929, in which both authors clearly sublimated the issues of construction to those of function and ergonometry. At that time, the authors were successors to a new generation of architects who, after World War I, were engaged in the social aspects of building and simultaneously in redefining furniture's tasks.

Experiments continue to this day. When design does not merely follow fashionable trends, industrial developments are utilized in the most varied ways—from High Tech to recycling. Thus, the optimal armchair, office chair, or car seat is again and again reinvented following the needs and possibilities of its time. The Post-Modern and, by now, post-industrial worlds offer us specialization and rich individualism; in *50 Chairs*, Mel Byars consciously pays tribute to both.

Alexander von Vegesack
Director
Vitra Design Museum
Weil am Rhein, Germany

Foreword:
Recent Technological Innovations
in Design and Materials

Sigfried Gideon argued in his book *Mechanization Takes Command* (1948) that the industrial world's material culture is continuously being affected by scientific and industrial progress. In his book, which offers an encompassing approach to design, he was first to claim that the anonymous contributions to science are as important as the history of individuals and design. Today, even though few of us know the inventors of new materials (for example, at Du Pont, Roy Plunkett discovered Teflon and Stephanie Kwolek, Kevlar), they are indeed not anonymous, merely little known.

In the middle of this century when Gideon was discussing the contributions of science to design, designers remained, as in previous centuries, committed to the "truth" of materials. More recently, Paola Antonelli, the associate curator of design at The Museum of Modern Art in New York City, became one of the first to recognize that designers today are turning from a devotion to the "truth" of materials as a traditional absolute value and an ideal standard. Her landmark exhibition in America and Japan—"Mutant Materials in Contemporary Design" (1995-96)—included examples, some in this volume, by contemporary designers who have customized, extended, or modified the physical universe of materials, quite differently so than in the past.

As a result of the use of new materials (like plastics, compounds and glues) as well as traditional ones (like wood and glass), the range of recent chair design has been remarkable, provoking the question, "Just how differently can one chair vary from another?" The answer is, "Very differently," encouraged by the essential structure of a chair which must include only a seating surface and a back; the stool, with only a seating surface, is a variant. These minimal criteria for a chair's construction favor infinite possibilities for chair configuration.

The 50 examples here were drawn from the plethora of the last decade and a half; in most cases, they were chosen for their innovatory characteristics and the manipulation of materials, often for recycling purposes.

A conscious effort was made to include the work of designers worldwide. However, most are male and European, particularly Italian, although there are also those from North and South America, Asia, Australia, and other countries in Europe. Yet, in attempting to represent the best of design today, an imbalance in the number of Italian designers and manufacturers was inevitable. In Italy, possibly uniquely among all other countries, the climate created by the symbiotic, if not always amicable, relationships among manufacturers, schools, publishers, the government, and native and immigrant designers has fostered the circumstances under which innovation, imagination, experimentation, and production have become fecund. Nevertheless, a global balance was assiduously attempted.

The chairs here, chosen as much for the use of materials as for the manipulation of them, are far from inclusive examples or even fully representational of the past 15 years. Rather, they were chosen for their variety. In selecting the objects, there was no assumption that anyone, in any culture or country, would wish to use any one of them at home or in the office. After all, most of us are still held in the fond embrace of things past, and the objects here very much represent the present. Unfortunately, Modernism—the 20th-century rejection of the restraining conservatism of prior centuries—has never adequately served the more nurturing aspects of the domestic environment that most of us desire. Modernism has frequently failed to cater to our physical needs (through softness and warmth) and our appetite for visual and intellectual stimulation (through surface variety and intricate images). And most of the chairs here indeed do not serve these basic demands; the cerebral stimulation provided by the examples is of an entirely different character.

Some of the objects may appear to be sheer folly. However, those which superficially seem to be merely comic have far more depth. The efforts are conjured by trained designers not only seriously aware of their responsibilities but also harbingers of inherited, nationally

Foreword

indigenous senses of humor which vary from country to country.

The categories into which the chairs are divided (see the Contents page) are arbitrary in that more than one material (for example, metal with wood) has more often than not been married to make them.

The layout of this book, intentionally accompanied by sparse text, illustrates how the furniture has been made, possibly the first book to cover this aspect as a primary theme. Design books, publications, and exhibitions rarely show us the details of how a piece of furniture is constructed; *Domus* magazine serves as an exception, but then not a consistent one. On the following pages, you will discover how the chairs were built and, with the skin removed in some examples, how their skeletons look. Examples include not only one-of-a-kind designs and short runs of 80 or fewer pieces, but also larger editions, such as the 700,000 or so seats produced from 1989-96 for the Mazda MX-5 "Miata" automobile (pages 152-155) and the 500,000 folding chairs designed by Gastone Rinaldi manufactured by Fly Line since 1980 (pages 142-145). The small editions as well as the maquettes for larger runs are testament to the Arts and Crafts tradition and approach, still practiced worldwide, having not yet fully been replaced by computer preproduction techniques. And, happily, the mass-produced work serves as proof that imagination and design excellence is permitted and even encouraged by some large-scale manufacturers.

The selections were based on my preferences, my personal guidelines for aesthetic and technological criteria, the availability of images that would fully illustrate an object, and the generosity and cooperation of designers and manufacturers, some providing photographs taken especially for the book.

The intention at the onset of planning this book project was to have no more than one chair by each designer represented, but, due to the rich output of Philippe Starck

and Alberto Meda and the imagination of the Campana brothers, the parameter was excused in these three cases.

You will find no histories of designers, no bibliographies, and no lengthy text or analysis, except of course this Foreword and Herr von Vegesack's Introduction. The chairs follow one another from 1 to 50, categorized according to the materials used or to articulation solutions.

50 Chairs will hopefully tweak your imagination, reveal the genius of certain trained designers, offer insights into the possible manipulation of new and traditional materials, question the boundary line, if there is one, between fine art and design, and, if nothing else, amuse and entertain.

Mel Byars
New York City

Wood

"Puzzle" armchair

Designer: David Kawecki (American, b. 1949)
Manufacturer: 3D: Interiors, San Francisco, California, U.S.A.
Date of design: 1991

This chair is laser cut in discrete sections, economically shipped flat, and assembled by the customer. It may be a bit of a problem discovering the proper sections to fit together, thus the name. Compare Kawecki's chair to Rietveld's "Armchair 'First Model' " (*Gerrit Th. Rietveld, The Complete Works*, Utrecht: Centraal Museum, 1992, no. 120).

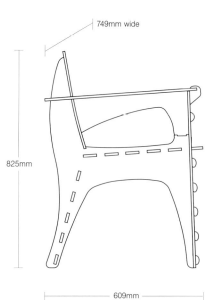

749mm wide

825mm

609mm

Laser cutting head.

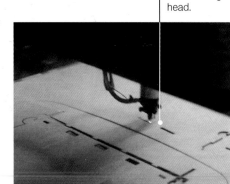

Viewed through a protective glass (left), the laser head cuts out the various parts of the chair from a sheet of 5-ply Baltic birch plywood (6mm thick). Instructions for the cutting pattern are provided by a computer program which directs the laser-cutting head, resulting in precisely fitting chair sections.

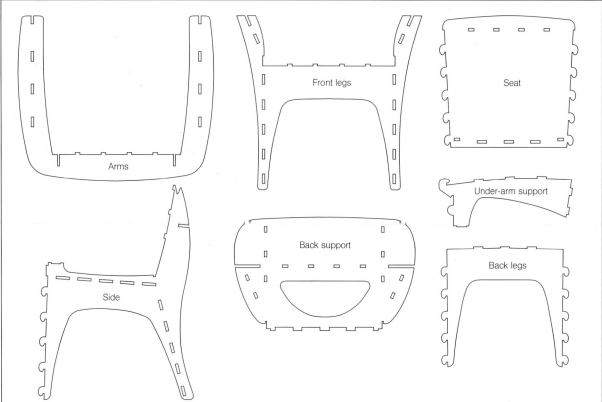

Arms

Front legs

Seat

Side

Back support

Under-arm support

Back legs

"Dry" side chair

Designer: Massimo Morozzi (Italian, b. 1941)
Manufacturer: Matrix, divisione della
Giorgetti S.p.A., Meda, Italy
Date of design 1987

For economical shipment and possibly even experimental purposes, the chair's assembly and disassembly is accomplished by a single winged bolt—no adhesives required. Available in polished or lacquered natural or in multi-color aniline-dyed beechwood with or without a seat cushion, the chair is composed of elements sawn with hand tools.

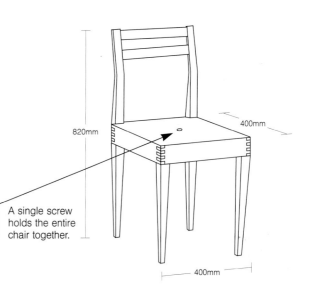

820mm

400mm

400mm

A single screw holds the entire chair together.

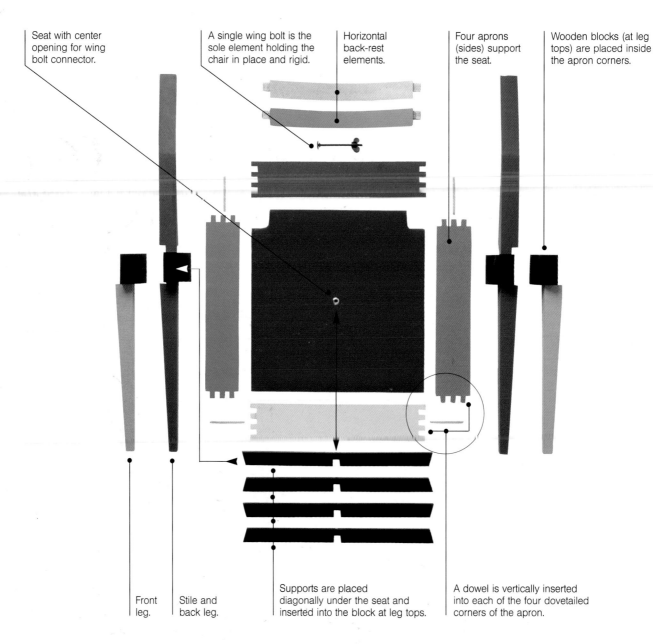

Seat with center opening for wing bolt connector.

A single wing bolt is the sole element holding the chair in place and rigid.

Horizontal back-rest elements.

Four aprons (sides) support the seat.

Wooden blocks (at leg tops) are placed inside the apron corners.

Front leg.

Stile and back leg.

Supports are placed diagonally under the seat and inserted into the block at leg tops.

A dowel is vertically inserted into each of the four dovetailed corners of the apron.

"Puzzle" stacking chair

Designer: Essaime (né Stéphane Millet, French, b. 1949)
Manufacturer: Quart de Poil', Paris, France.
Date of design: 1994

For domestic, office, or public use, the chair can be ganged at the sides for multiple use side-by-side and at the floor for multiple use in rows. It is designed in side-chair and armchair versions and exhibits a bit more aestheic flare than most public seating.

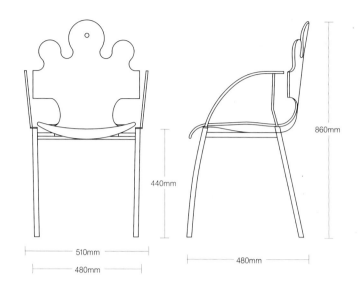

440mm
510mm
480mm
860mm
480mm

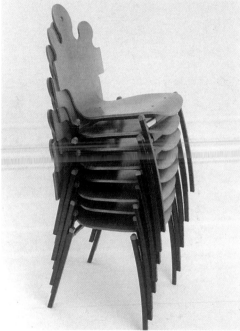

Stackable for storage.

Floor links for the ganged configuration are available colored to match the floor covering.

Two-way bent stained and varnished beechwood-veneered plywood.

Matching, stained beechwood tips fill in the tops of the extruded steel legs.

Extruded steel legs and horizontal supports (2mm x 2mm) are varnished black.

Seat/back is screwed onto the frame in three places: two onto the front, one in the back.

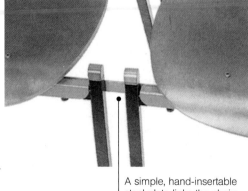

A simple, hand-insertable steel plate links the chairs sideways.

Wood/17

"Chair 9"

Designers: James Davis (British, b. 1965)
and David Walley (Australian, b. 1960)
Manufacturer: Yellow Diva, London, Great Britain
Date of design: 1994

With the outward appearance of being hot-wire cut from a piece of synthetic foam, the chair is actually quite intricate and hollow inside with Pirelli rubber webbing providing springy support. The webbing is in turn covered over with a layer of reconstituted foam and thence by dacron and finally over both layers of padding is the upholstery material.

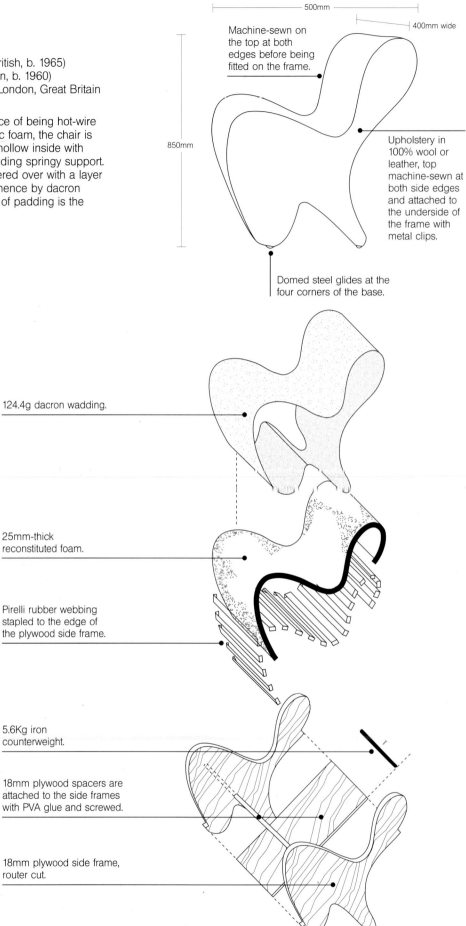

Machine-sewn on the top at both edges before being fitted on the frame.

500mm

400mm wide

850mm

Upholstery in 100% wool or leather, top machine-sewn at both side edges and attached to the underside of the frame with metal clips.

Domed steel glides at the four corners of the base.

124.4g dacron wadding.

25mm-thick reconstituted foam.

Pirelli rubber webbing stapled to the edge of the plywood side frame.

5.6Kg iron counterweight.

18mm plywood spacers are attached to the side frames with PVA glue and screwed.

18mm plywood side frame, router cut.

Wood/21

"Cross Check" armchair

Designer: Frank Gehry (Canadian, b. 1929)
Manufacturer: The Knoll Group, East Greenville, Pennsylvania
Date of design: 1992

The architect/designer, with project designer Daniel Sachs and design technician Tom MacMichael, spent over 24 months and a large sum of the manufacturer's money on the development of a group of bentwood furniture. The chair's major feature may lie in its use of a newly developed glue which eliminates the necessity of metal fasteners of any kind. The "Cross Check" armchair is one in a group of chairs, two tables, and an ottoman, available in clear or ebonized finishes.

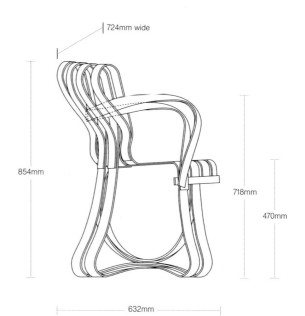

724mm wide
854mm
718mm
470mm
632mm

The design concept was inspired by the wood-strip bushel basket made popular by fruit growers in the 19th and 20th centuries.

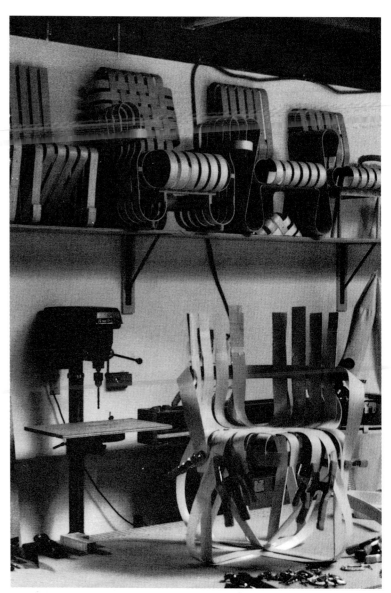

In a workshop near the architect/designer's office in Venice, California, 115 prototypes were produced over a period of about two years.

No. 6 continued ▶

"Cross Check" armchair

The lengthy experimentation time resulted in five chairs, an ottoman, and two tables being placed into production.

The strips (50mm wide x 2mm thick) are made of 6-, 7-, or 8-ply hard white maplewood, bonded with high-bonding urea glue. For resilience, the wood grain runs lengthwise.

No assembly glues are used on the woven seat, facilitating a springy flex.

Newly developed thermoset assembly glue provides structural rigidity and eliminates the need for metal fasteners.

A prototype bending form illustrates how the wooden strips were folded in place.

An early version of the "Hat Trick" side chair (1991).

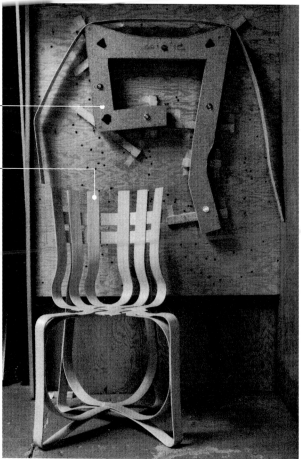

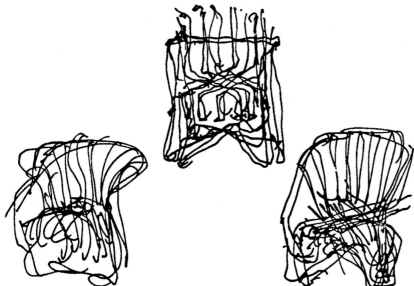

The designer's study (1990) for the "Cross Check" armchair.

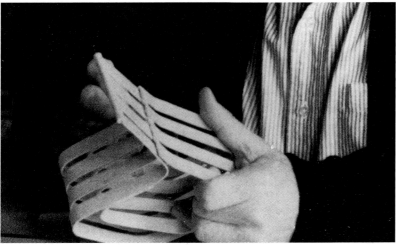

The designer's earliest (1989) experiment in manipulating maplewood strips.

Ca. 1989, the designer holds a maquette of the "High Sticking" side chair (1991).

"Less" stacking side chair and stool

Designer: Marco Ferreri (Italian, b. 1958)
Manufacturer: BPA International, Cabiate (CO),
Italy
Date of design: 1993

The use of advanced technology in this chair
lies not in its minimal form but rather in the
construction of the "upholstery" on the seat and
the back rest. A layer of Softwood™, placed over
the padding, behaves like upholstery fabric.

Stacking configuration of the chair, available with a
beechwood frame, clear or black painted. Seat and
backrest are clear, medium gray, blue, orange, or green.

Plan view of the stacking
configuration of the stool.
Five examples shown here.

The top surface of the seat
(Softwood) is soft and
pliable, almost like fabric.

No. 7 continued ▶

"Less" stacking side chair and stool

175mm
140mm
765mm
450mm

405mm
350mm

463.5mm

Base wood surface.

Inner layer of fabric, combined with a layer of polyurethane foam, is bonded by high heat and pressure to the Softwood surface.

Softwood (top layer) acts as a soft upholstery material much like fabric.

The backrest is fitted into the stiles through slots (6mm wide) and riveted.

Parts of the superstructure are glued together, and the seat and backrest are held by eight bolts and eight screw rivets.

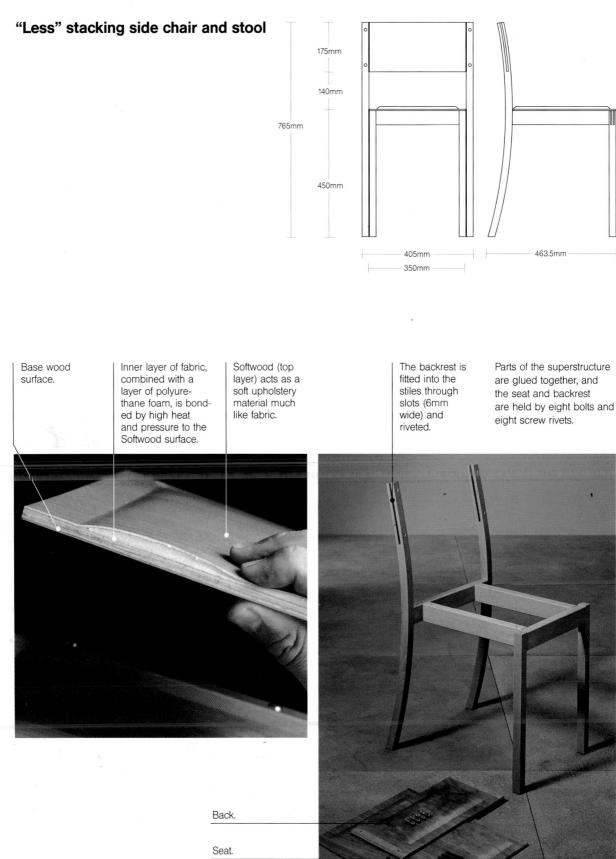

Back.

Seat.

"NXT" stacking chair

Designer: Peter Karpf (Danish, b. 1940)
Manufacturer: Swedese, Vaggeryd, Sweden (to 1996); Inredningsform, Malmö, Sweden (from 1996)
Date of design: 1991

Development of a patented process through intense research has resulted in the achievement of great strength and little weight in this chair through the fusion of very thin layers of a natural material—wood—at alternating grain angles. Weighing just 3.5Kg, the chair is available in a natural-wood finish and red, blue, yellow, or green lacquer colors.

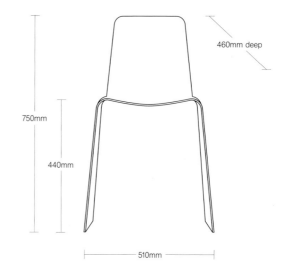

460mm deep

750mm

440mm

510mm

Back view of the "NXT" chair which is capable of being ganged through the use of a metal rod inserted through the legs and of being numbered with small discs.

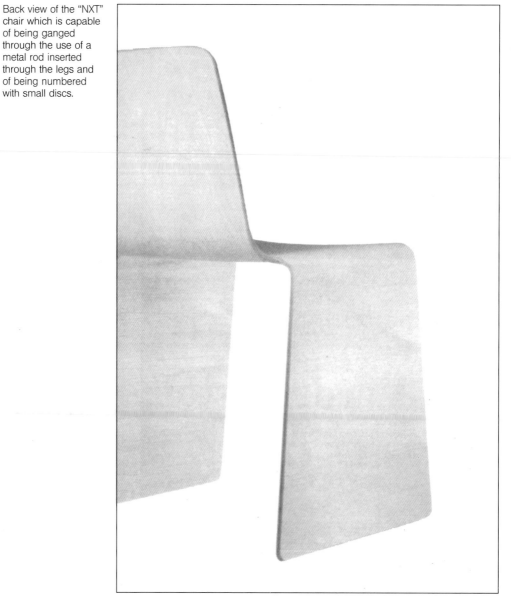

No. 8 continued ▶

"NXT" stacking chair

The radiating directional lines indicate the distribution of the occupant's weight which results from the four alternating grain layers on eight fused plywood sheets.

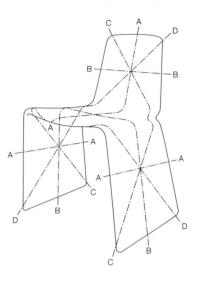

Arrows indicate grain direction of the A and B layers of veneer (see layer drawing below).

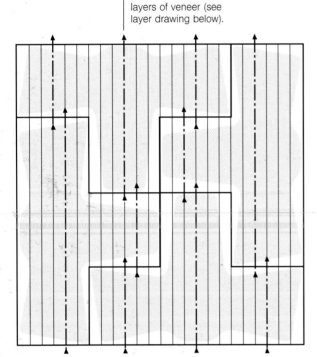

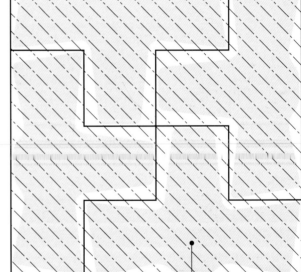

Flat sheets (above, left and right), before gluing, cutting, and heat-and-high-pressure bending.

Dotted lines (above) indicate grain direction of the C and D layers of veneer (see below).

Tan shapes indicate the flat cut-out shape before bending.

The eight alternating grain directions in the lamination sequence of one chair:

A: Top to bottom (180°)
B: Left to right (90°)
C: Diagonally left (45°)
D: Diagonally right (45°)
C: Diagonally left (45°)
D: Diagonally right (45°)
B: Left to right (90°)
A: Top to bottom (180°)

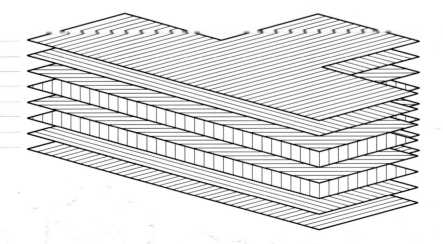

Metals

"Ota Otanek" chair

Designer: Bořek Šípek (Czechoslovakian, b. 1949)
Manufacturer: Vitra GmbH, Weil am Rhein, Germany
Date of design: 1988

Combining many of the qualities of fine traditional furniture of the centuries past with modern techniques, the materials in this chair include beaten copper, partially hand-worked wood, and steel. The manufacturer assembles the parts (made to the designer's specifications) fabricated by various outside suppliers. Perhaps the challenge assumed by the designer, as well as the manufacturer, was to produce an industrial object with the appearance of being handhewn; however, the chair is neither truly industrial nor fully handmade.

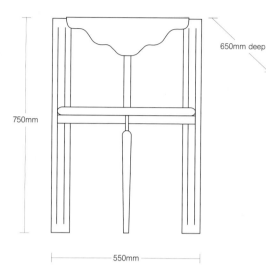

650mm deep

750mm

550mm

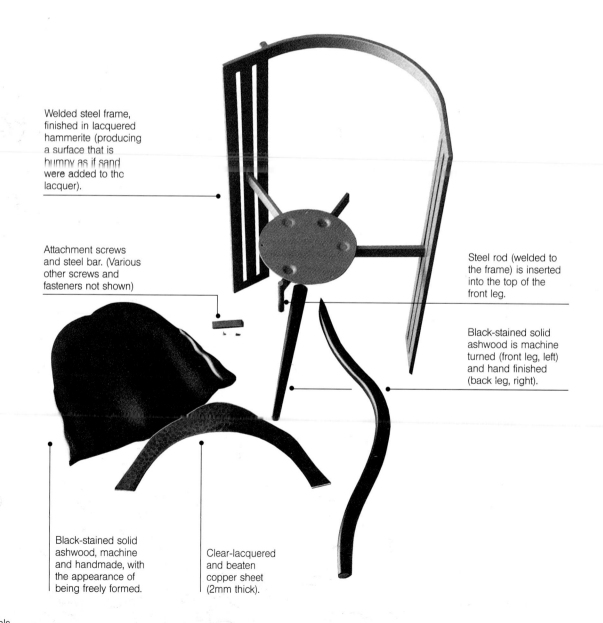

Welded steel frame, finished in lacquered hammerite (producing a surface that is bumpy as if sand were added to the lacquer).

Attachment screws and steel bar. (Various other screws and fasteners not shown)

Steel rod (welded to the frame) is inserted into the top of the front leg.

Black-stained solid ashwood is machine turned (front leg, left) and hand finished (back leg, right).

Black-stained solid ashwood, machine and handmade, with the appearance of being freely formed.

Clear-lacquered and beaten copper sheet (2mm thick).

"Mirandolina" stacking chair

Designer: Pietro Arosio (Italian, b. 1946)
Manufacturer: Zanotta S.p.A.,
Nova Milanese (MI), Italy.
Date of design: 1992

Like Marcel Breuer's aluminum chair of 1932-34 with the legs and the body as one piece of metal, this version is truly a whole one-piece chair, with no separate cross slats for the seat as in the Breuer version. Also, unlike Breuer's, the chair is inexpensive and light weight. The version here is an example of the kind of symbiotic relationship among designer, manufacturer, and materials' supplier which results in a successful, imaginative product.

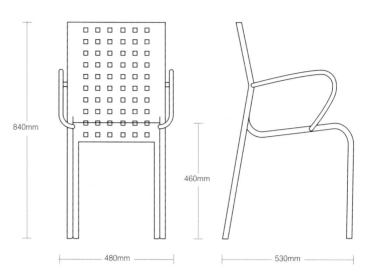

840mm
460mm
480mm
530mm

The armchair version features solid, extruded, square, bent aluminum arms, bolted to the seat and the back.

Metallic-stove-enameled aluminum alloy (3mm thick) for outdoor use, in metallic clear, black, green, light blue, or custom colors.

1250mm

Production process:

1. Only one firm in Italy can supply a 400mm-width extruded aluminum-alloy sheet (3mm thick).

2. The flat sheet is cut to size, including notching for the legs. The front and back legs are integral to the body; there is no welding.

3. The holes are punched out of the flat sheet to create a lighter weight and appearance.

4. Bending and shaping occurs in an hydraulic press.

5. The aluminum is painted in a small range of colors.

Sequential images show the pre-trimmed sheet (with the grid pattern already stamped out) being shaped by the hydraulic press.

"Mirò" chair

Designer: Carlo Forcolini (Italian, b. 1947)
Manufacturer: Alias S.r.l., Grumello del Monte (BG), Italy
Date of design: 1989

Exploiting the flexible nature of tempered steel, this spare, imaginative chair is painted in a Calder palette: the primary colors, black, white, and also silver. The structure eliminates traditional metal joinery. When viewed at a raked angle, the seat appears to have the silhouette of lips.

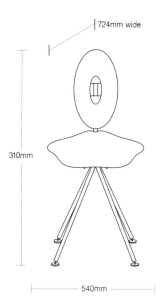

724mm wide

310mm

540mm

The drawing includes the backrest.

Seat is laser-cut malleable steel sheeting (2mm thick).

Steel tubular frame is 18mm diameter (1.5mm wall thickness) with glides at the floor connected to the tubular leg by thin metal rods.

Hollow tubular frame extension is capped closed.

Frame is assembled with stainless-steel nuts and bolts.

Shock absorber under the seat is expanded polyurethane (30Kg/m² density) and glued to the frame's end finial.

The malleable-steel seat is sprung from its leading edge beneath the front of the frame.

A bar-stool version is available with a foot-rest stretcher to stabilize the long, thin legs.

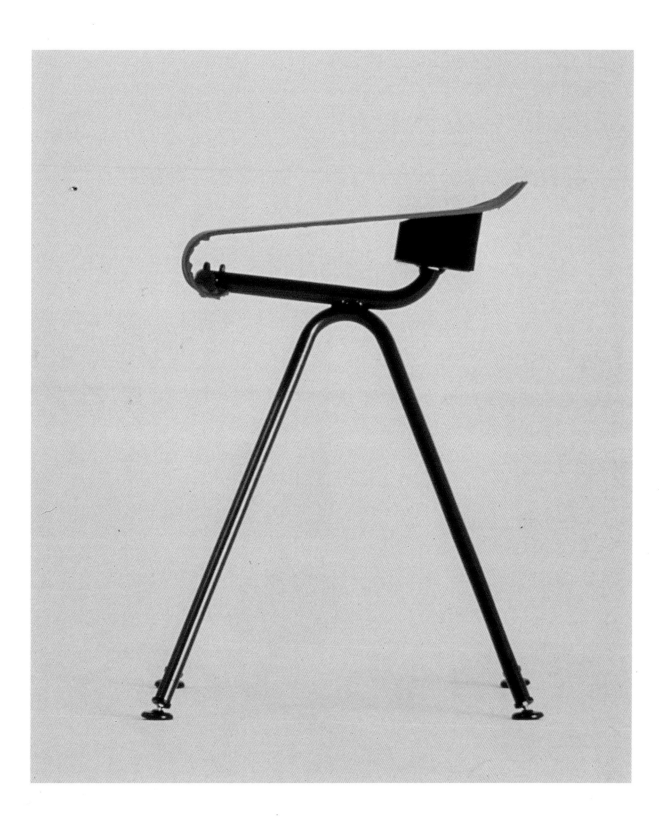

Metals/39

"Utility" side chair

Designer: Stephen Povey (British, b. 1951)
Manufacturer: Diametrics, London, England
Date of design: 1986

This chair is formed of standard tubular steel for the frame and legs and rubber-like suction cups for the ferrules. Assigning an everyday, ordinary product to a new use, the seat and back are dustbin (trash can) lids purchased by the designer-manufacturer directly from a dustbin producer in England. Excluding the suction cups, the chair is composed of only four pieces.

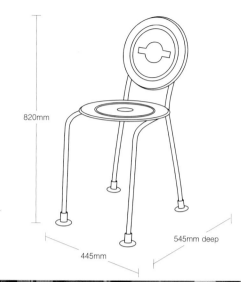

820mm
445mm
545mm deep

The designer arc-welds the frame to the seat—a very simple assembly.

The four parts (back, seat, and legs) are spray painted with stove enameled polyester powder.

Dustbin lid (328mm diameter) for the back supplied by Griffin Bros., England.

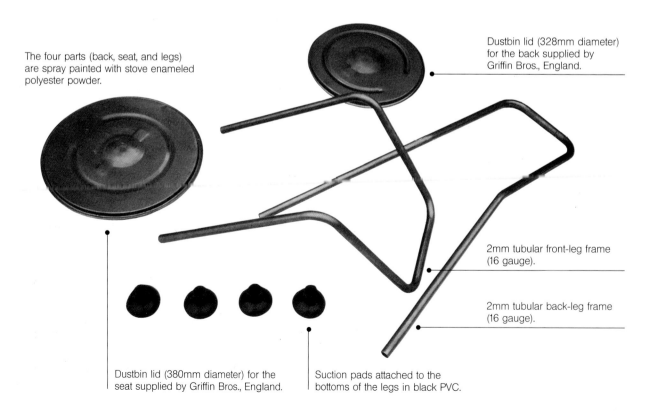

2mm tubular front-leg frame (16 gauge).

2mm tubular back-leg frame (16 gauge).

Dustbin lid (380mm diameter) for the seat supplied by Griffin Bros., England.

Suction pads attached to the bottoms of the legs in black PVC.

13

"How High the Moon" armchair

Designer: Shiro Kuramata (Japanese, 1934-1991)
Manufacturer: Vitra GmbH, Weil am Rhein,
Germany
Date of design: 1986-87

The leading representative of minimalism in
design at the time of his death, Kuramata
produced this chair as an artistic rather than
a functional composition, in punctured,
stretched steel. It is claimed by its manufacturer
to be the lightest large chair ever designed.

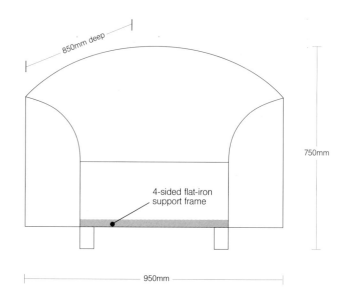

850mm deep

750mm

4-sided flat-iron
support frame

950mm

Solid steel templates are
used to cut the specially
treated steel mesh into
nine sections (plus the legs)
and the thin four-sided frame.

Parts of the chair are clamped and fixed
into place.

With sections of the chair touching at the
edges, the workman solders the sections at
the intersecting points of the mesh.

Sections of the chair are steadied using
a steel matrix.

A workman solders the top of the right
front to the tops of the arm and side.

About 2,300 soldering connections are
made on each chair before it is tuned to
eliminate twisting, then plated with 15μ of
nickel and, finally, coated with an epoxy resin.

"Billboard" chair

Designer: Maurizio Favetta (Italian, b. 1959)
Manufacturer: King Size by Lasar, Milano, Italy
Date of design: 1993

Far more serious than a quick glance may
reveal, the design accommodates photographs,
sections of posters, fabrics, colored paper,
graphics, or other thin flat images, which
should be trimmed to the precise size of the
back section for best effect.

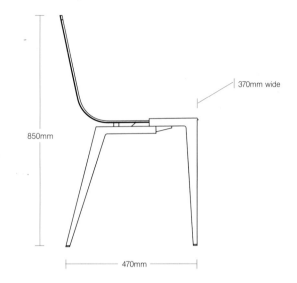

A snap-on leather padded
section (not shown) covers
the screws which hold the
leg-frame sections together
and also the leading edge
(point A) of the sloping back.

Leg-frame sections in cast
aluminum, enamel-painted
in black, silver, red, or blue.
The two sections are inserted into one another and
held by hex-headed screws.

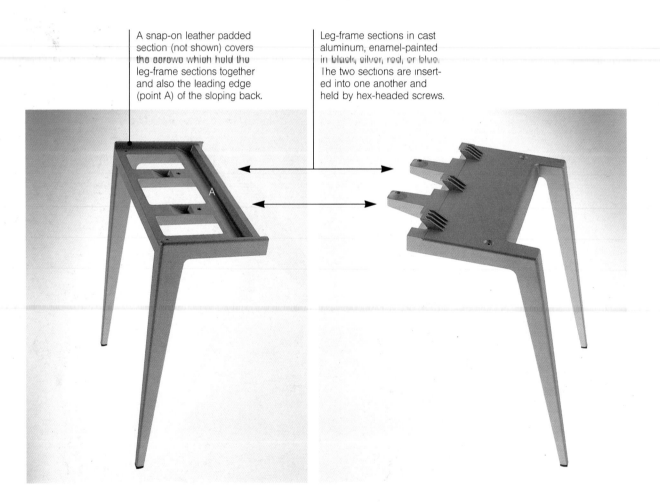

No. 14 continued ▶

"Billboard" chair

Three angled elements, as part of the top of the front-leg unit, elevate the curved seat from the base, creating an airy effect when seen from the side.

Two polyvinyl discs, placed on the top of the back-leg unit, elevate the back of the seat from the base.

An image or flat material (trimmed to 370 x 640mm) is sandwiched between a sheet of clear acrylic and the bent aluminum back and flows downward onto the back of the seat.

Polyvinyl glides are inserted into a key opening through the side of the cast aluminum legs (rather than the traditional method of insertion through the ends where the glides may fall out and become lost).

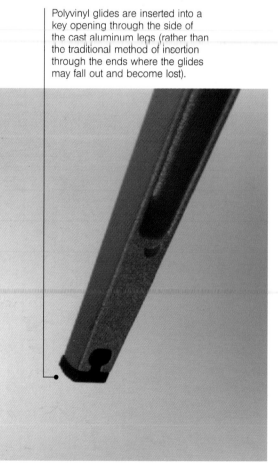

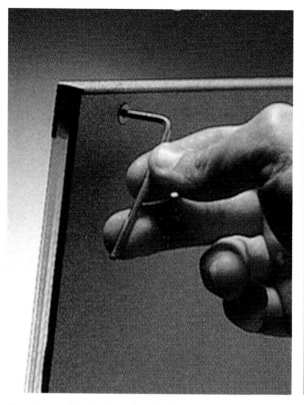

The clear acrylic sheet covering the aluminum back rest is removed with the hex screw driver provided with the chair.

The head rail is removed so that the artwork can be slid between the aluminum back rest and the clear acrylic covering.

The aluminum back rest.

The artwork, trimmed to 370 x 640mm and no thicker than 1mm, is sandwiched between the clear acrylic sheet and the aluminum back.

The clear acrylic sheet fits into the back edge of the leather-covered seat and is screwed into the top of the aluminum back rest.

Discs chair

Designers: Fernando Campana (Brazilian, b. 1961)
and Humberto Campana (Brazilian, b. 1953)
Manufacturer: Campana Objetos Ltda,
São Paulo/SP, Brazil.
Date of design: 1992

A freely formed seat that questions the standard
approach to chair design. Neither the technology
(sawing, welding, metal bending) nor the materials
(wood and steel) are particularly advanced but the
depth of imagination is undeniable. The chair is
one of a kind, but, even so, additional copies
would all be somehow varied.

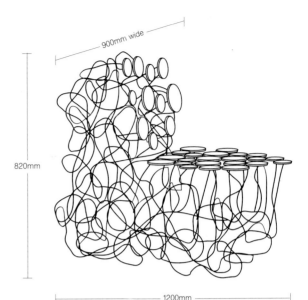

900mm wide

820mm

1200mm

Since the chair is handmade, dimensions are approximate.

Steel rod (10 cm diame-
ter) is bent by hand in
a free-form manner.

11 discs in pinewood in two
sizes for the backrest and
22 others for the seat.

Steel discs (50 cm diameter, welded to the
ends of the bent steel rods) are screwed to
the backsides of the pinewood disc.

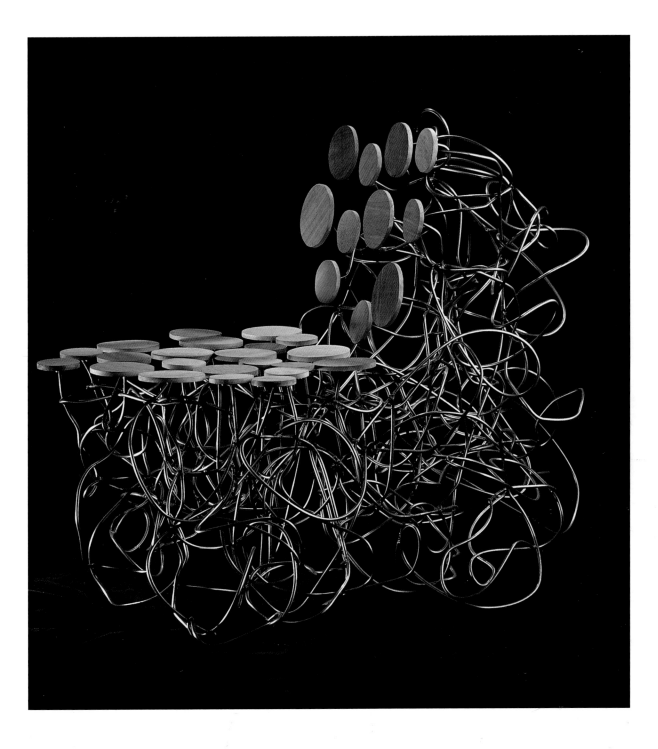

"Well Tempered" armchair

Designers: Ron Arad (Israeli, b. 1951)
Manufacturer: Vitra GmbH, Weil am Rhein,
Germany
Date of design: 1986-87

Known for his one-of-a-kind chairs in beaten
metal, this design in tempered steel (thus,
the title) is an example of a less-handhewned,
more rational form of his work. Very simple
and with a delightful springiness, the chair is
composed of only four pieces.

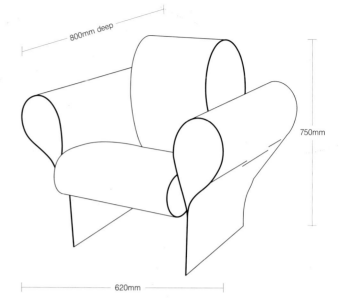

High-grade steel (1mm thick).

Wing nuts hold the sections together. No
welding or adhesives are employed.

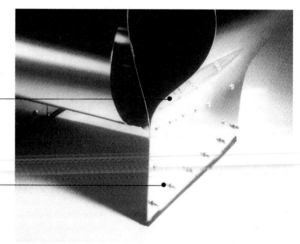

An outline pattern (right)
was entered into a
computer which controlled
the tracking of a laser-
burning machine. The
holes (for the wing nuts for
assembly) were drilled by
hand using a template.

To prevent scratching
of the shinny surface, a protective white plastic foil is
left on the steel sheet until it
reaches the customer.

The side sections are
crimped (indicated by the
broken lines, right) by a
bending machine at a 90°
angle.

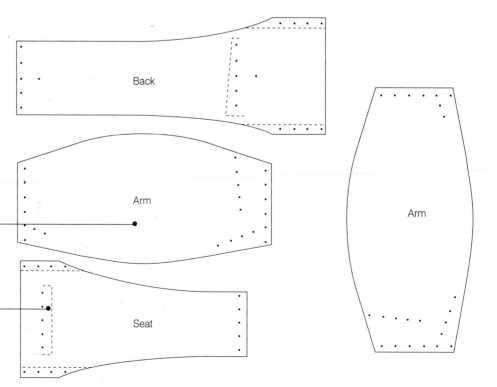

Back

Arm

Arm

Seat

Aluminum stacking chair and stool

Designers: Piet Hein Eek (Dutch, b. 1967)
and Nob Ruijgrok (Dutch, b. 1966)
Manufacturer: Eek en Ruijgrok vof, Geldrop,
The Netherlands
Date of design: 1994

A practical, inexpensive, and very light-weight seat,
produced with computer punching and bending
machines, was also designed in a stacking-stool
version. Made solely of bent aluminum sheeting
with the exception of self-sealing plastic pop-nails
for assembly.

Composed of seven sections,
the anodized aluminum sheet
is 2mm thick.

Section 1:
Front side of back rest.

Section 2:
Seat.

Section 7:
Back side of the back rest
which extends from the seat.

Sections 3-6:
Four legs (center and at
the right and bottom).

Aluminum chair and stool

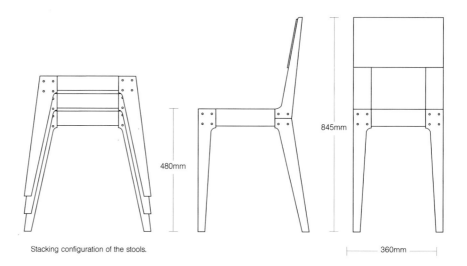

480mm

845mm

360mm

Stacking configuration of the stools.

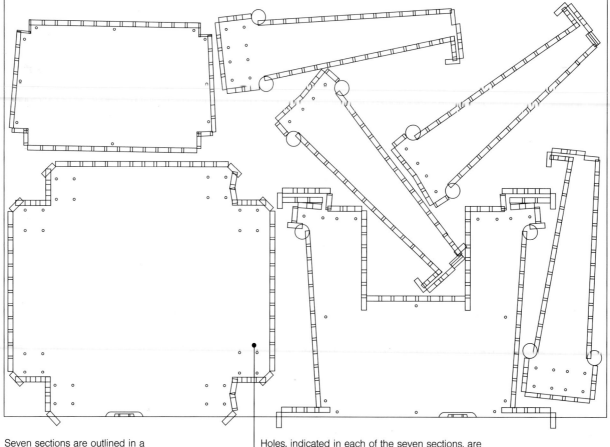

Seven sections are outlined in a drawing used for a computer-controlled punching machine and bending machine.

Holes, indicated in each of the seven sections, are punched at the same time each section is punched out of an anodized aluminum sheet. Non-removable punch-nails are used in the assembly.

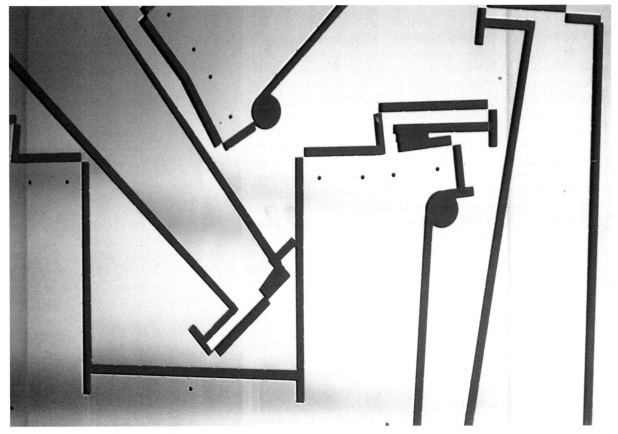

Cut-out sections, including the negative refuse, before bending.

"L'aube et le temps qu'elle dure" ("Dawn and the Time It Lasts") stacking chair

Designer: Sylvain Dubuisson (French, b. 1946)
Manufacturer: L.C.S.D., Le Pin, France
Date of design: 1987

A departure from the archetypal 4-legged chair, this example was produced in two sheet-aluminum sections. The chair was made in an edition of three for the exhibition "Tandem," held in Romans-sur-Isère, France. The title, used by art historian François Barré in an essay which inspired the designer, was originally conjured by Jules Renard. Compare the chair to the example on pages 30–32.

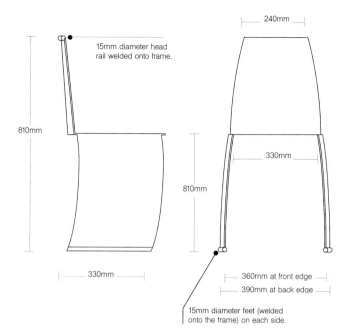

15mm diameter head rail welded onto frame.

240mm

810mm

810mm

330mm

330mm

360mm at front edge

390mm at back edge

15mm diameter feet (welded onto the frame) on each side.

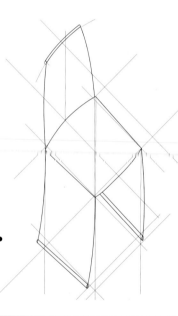

Projection drawing by the designer.

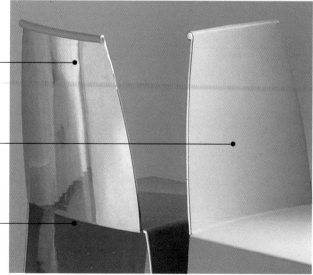

Aluminum AG3 (4mm thick) is cut, rolled, folded, and, on the back side, polished.

Green-dyed leather is glued to the surface of the aluminum on one side.

The chair is made in two parts: the back is welded to the seat-legs unit.

"Armonica" side chair

Designers: Herbert Ohl (German, b. 1926)
and Jutta Ohl (German, b. 1938)
Manufacturer: Matteograssi S.p.A.,
Mariano Comense (CO), Italy
Date of design: 1991

Herbert Ohl claims that most chairs create "health-endangering" effects on their occupants. This chair, called a "seating tool" by its ambitious creators, purportedly offers free, "harmonic" movement which in turn lends "rhythmic dynamics" to one's "body and life," in the designer's own words. Movement is realized through the malleable characteristic of the metal pedestal.

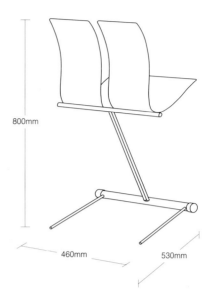

800mm

460mm   530mm

All joints are force fused. No welding and no adhesives are employed for joining. The leather covering on the metal surface of the seat and back is coated. The baked metal surfaces are finished with a choice of polyester epoxy, or powdered epoxy, paint in film thicknesses of 120-180 microns.

Leather-covered, molded tempered steel (2mm thickness).

Aluminum tubing (25mm diameter) with end caps in black PVC.

Leather-covered, molded tempered steel (3mm thickness).

Pedestal of two separate steel rods (12mm diameter each, 489mm high) with an elastic characteristic.

Aluminum-tube base (25mm diameter) fitted with black PVC caps.

"Donut" glides in black PVC (31mm diameter).

Steel rod (12mm diameter) with an elastic characteristic.

Black PVC caps.

"Dakota" armchair

Designer: Paolo Rizzatto (Italian, b. 1941)
Manufacturer: Cassina S.p.A., Meda (MI), Italy
Date of design: 1995

This chair features a cast-aluminum seat
shell which accommodates either four
straight legs or a swivel pedestal. The
inner upholstery, with its special design
of fingers and a plastic track attachment,
is removable and replaceable.

The two versions (straight legs or pedestal)
are available in:
• Completely upholstered in saddle leather
and chair trim in soft leather.
• Saddle leather outside and removable
fabric cover inside with soft leather trim.
• Completely upholstered with removable
fabric cover with trim in same fabric.

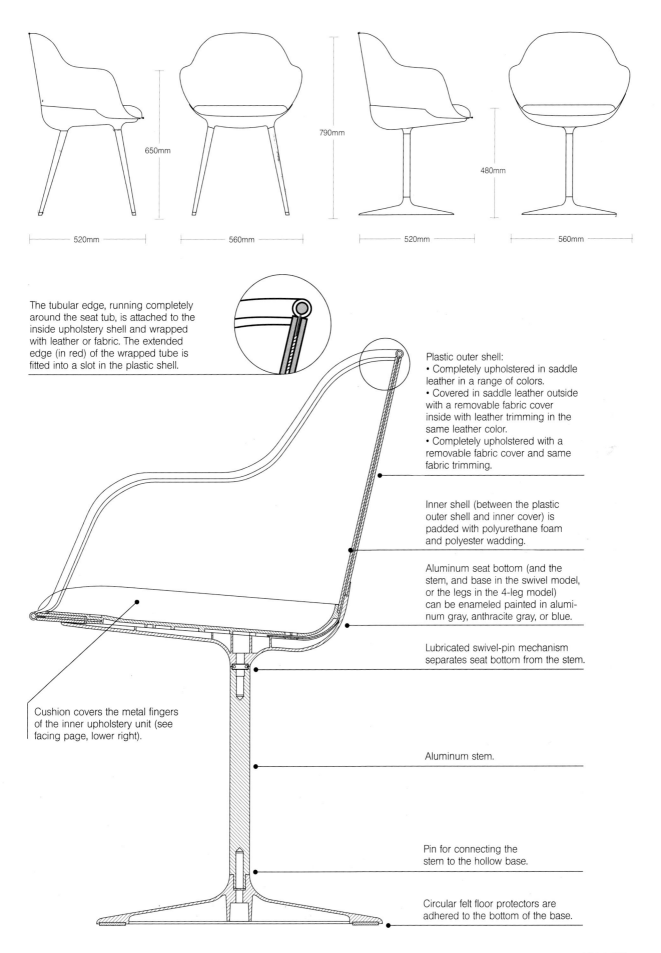

650mm

790mm

480mm

520mm   560mm   520mm   560mm

The tubular edge, running completely around the seat tub, is attached to the inside upholstery shell and wrapped with leather or fabric. The extended edge (in red) of the wrapped tube is fitted into a slot in the plastic shell.

Plastic outer shell:
• Completely upholstered in saddle leather in a range of colors.
• Covered in saddle leather outside with a removable fabric cover inside with leather trimming in the same leather color.
• Completely upholstered with a removable fabric cover and same fabric trimming.

Inner shell (between the plastic outer shell and inner cover) is padded with polyurethane foam and polyester wadding.

Aluminum seat bottom (and the stem, and base in the swivel model, or the legs in the 4-leg model) can be enameled painted in aluminum gray, anthracite gray, or blue.

Lubricated swivel-pin mechanism separates seat bottom from the stem.

Cushion covers the metal fingers of the inner upholstery unit (see facing page, lower right).

Aluminum stem.

Pin for connecting the stem to the hollow base.

Circular felt floor protectors are adhered to the bottom of the base.

"Longframe" chaise longue and "Armframe" easy chair

Designer: Alberto Meda (Italian, b. 1945)
Manufacturer: Alias S.r.l., Grumello del Monte (BG), Italy
Date of design: 1993

An amalgamation of visual and physical lightness has been incorporated into a lounge seat appropriate for indoor or outdoor use. The result may be more an engineering accomplishment than an aesthetic one. The net upholstery is held in place by covered plastic piping which is fed into the channel of the side frame. The Kevlar cord stretched among the legs controls the frame's twisting.

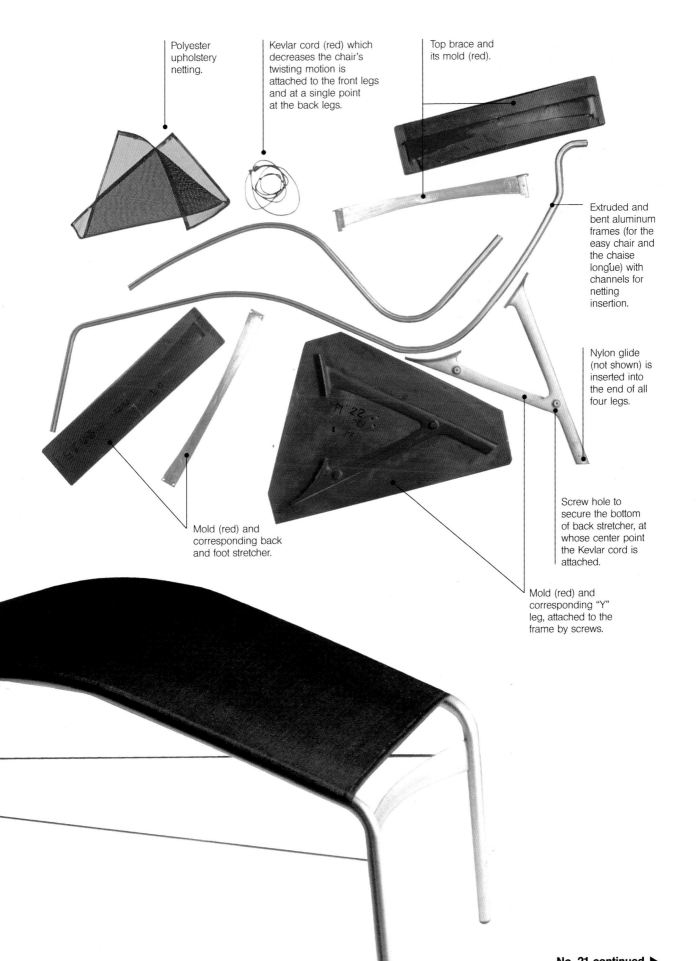

Polyester upholstery netting.

Kevlar cord (red) which decreases the chair's twisting motion is attached to the front legs and at a single point at the back legs.

Top brace and its mold (red).

Extruded and bent aluminum frames (for the easy chair and the chaise longue) with channels for netting insertion.

Nylon glide (not shown) is inserted into the end of all four legs.

Screw hole to secure the bottom of back stretcher, at whose center point the Kevlar cord is attached.

Mold (red) and corresponding back and foot stretcher.

Mold (red) and corresponding "Y" leg, attached to the frame by screws.

No. 21 continued ▶

"Long-frame" chaise longue and "Armframe" easy chair

No Kevlar cord nor upper back stretcher are used in the "Armframe" version (left). The extruded aluminum frame design, into which the hem of the taut polyester netting is fed at the inside edges, eliminates the necessity of being attached at top and bottom edges.

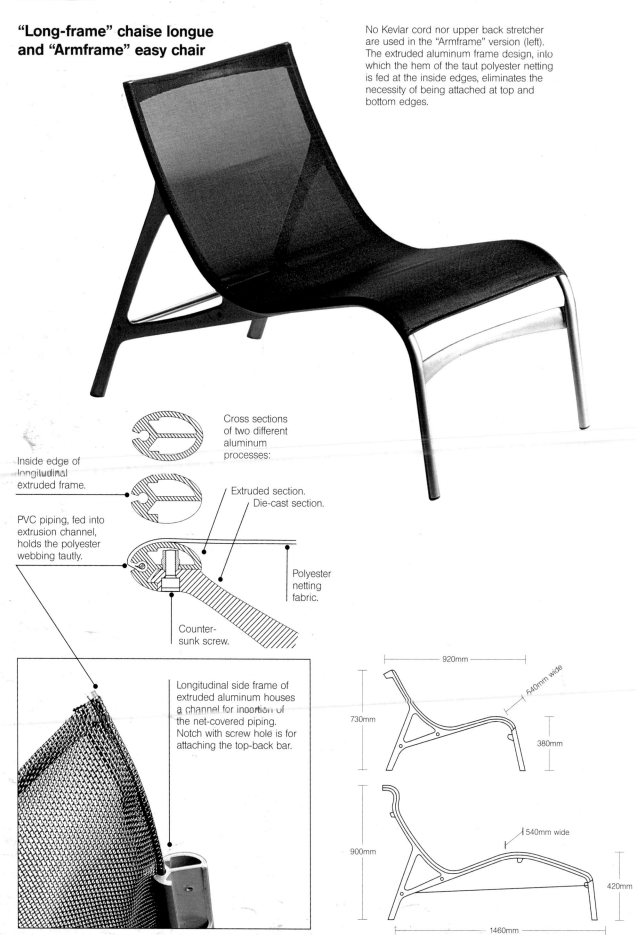

Cross sections of two different aluminum processes:

Inside edge of longitudinal extruded frame.

Extruded section.
Die-cast section.

PVC piping, fed into extrusion channel, holds the polyester webbing tautly.

Polyester netting fabric.

Countersunk screw.

Longitudinal side frame of extruded aluminum houses a channel for insertion of the net-covered piping. Notch with screw hole is for attaching the top-back bar.

920mm
540mm wide
730mm
380mm

900mm
540mm wide
420mm
1460mm

Plastics

"LAM L 1000" chair system

Designers: Roberto Lucci (Italian, b. 1942) and
Paolo Orlandini (Italian, b. 1941)
Manufacturer: Shelby Williams Industries,
Morristown, Tennessee, U.S.A.
Date of design: 1991

On most ergonomic chairs, the seat can be
raised and lowered. But, unlike others, there are
no springs or gas pistons on this chair. A simple
self-adjusting tilt configuration makes the chair
economical and reliable. The system (of which
about 60,000 examples a year have been
produced since 1992) includes models with
four legs, sled legs, and a swivel pedestal and
attached to a bar for public tandem seating. The
designers sometimes closely collaborate but in
separate offices, while at other times they com-
pete with each other on the same project.

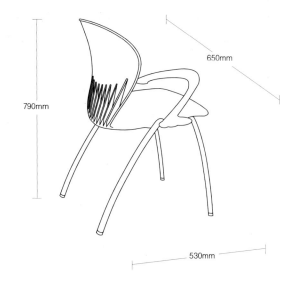

Of the numerous configurations, the 4-leg armchair
is shown in the drawing here.

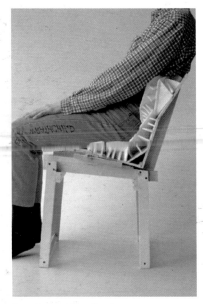

Experimental ergonomic mock-up.

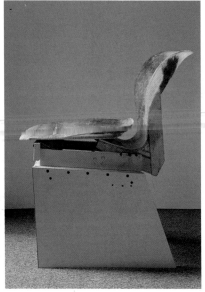

Full-size model in glass reinforced polyester.

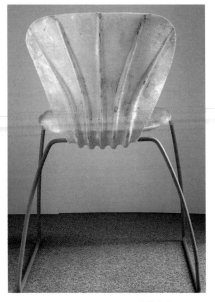

On another model in glass reinforced
polyester, the fins (running the full
height of the back) were increased in
number but shortened in the final version.

The lever principle which synchronizes
the back and seat movement is
illustrated through a 3-dimensional
model (right).

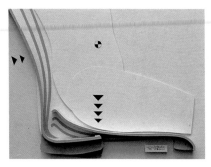

Using paper and PVC tubing in
a full-size model (right), the most
desirable proportions are sought.

No. 22 continued ▶

"LAM L 1000" chair system

Models available in the seating system:

4-leg side chair.
4-leg armchair (preceding page).
Sled-base side chair (below left).
Sled-base armchair (below right).
Swivel chair.
Swivel armchair.
Modular seating.

4-leg model:
Bent and stamped
steel tubing (25mm
diameter).

Swivel model:
Bent and stamped
steel tubing
(30mm diameter).

Polyamide
roll
casters.

The fins on the
back permit self tilting.
The material does not
split where the back
meets the seat.

Fireproof, injection-
molded, recyclable
polypropylene resin,
available in a
range of colors.

The back and seat are available
in bare plastic or with foam-
rubber and polypropylene pads
covered with fabric or PVC
material.

Bent and stamped steel tubing
(18mm diameter), powdered epoxy
finishes (two standard colors).

"Drop" stool

Designer: Frans Van Praet (Belgian, b. 1937)
Manufacturer: Metcator-Orteliushuis,
Antwerp, Belgium
Date of design: 1994-95

Combining the technologies of metal
bending and plastic casting, this geo-
metrically sophisticated form can be
used both out- and indoors. Any one
of eight colors is available, including
different combinations for seat and base.

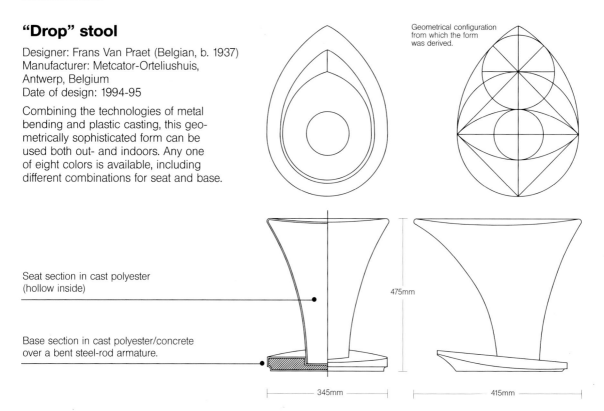

Geometrical configuration
from which the form
was derived.

Seat section in cast polyester
(hollow inside)

Base section in cast polyester/concrete
over a bent steel-rod armature.

475mm

345mm

415mm

Cast polyester (hollow inside)

A bent steel-rod armature and sleeve
reinforces the polyester/concrete
cast base.

The two sections (seat and base)
are coated in one of eight colors
and glued together.

"AC1" swivel chair

Designer: Antonio Citterio (Italian, b. 1950)
Manufacturer: Vitra GmbH, Weil am Rhein, Germany
Date of design: 1988

Part of a coordinated collection of desks, bookshelves, and other furnishings for the business office, this chair adjusts to the occupant's body, following the body's movements, and flexes in a number of ways. Many of its parts, traditionally in metal, are in plastics.

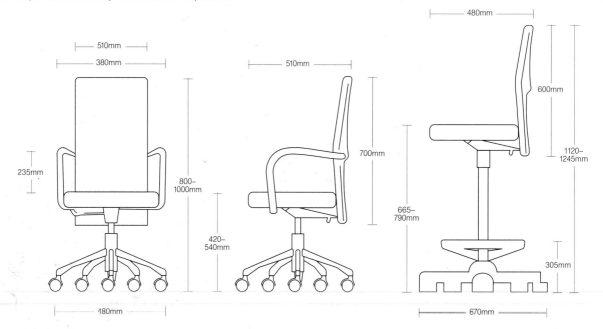

Through the use of flexible Delrin (a plastic material used for the back rest) and a synchronized mechanism beneath the seat, the seat and the flexing back rest are automatically adjusted when the occupant leans forward or pushes back.

The flexing back (covered in leather) of Paolo Deganello's "Documenta" chair (1987), also produced by Vitra, was the inspiration for the design of the flexing back of Citterio's "AC1" chair.

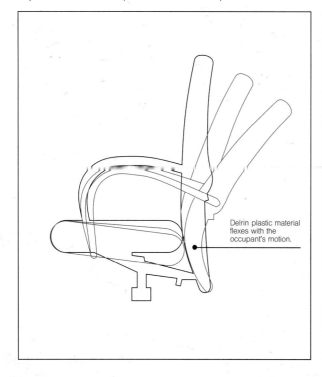

Delrin plastic material flexes with the occupant's motion.

"AC1" swivel chair

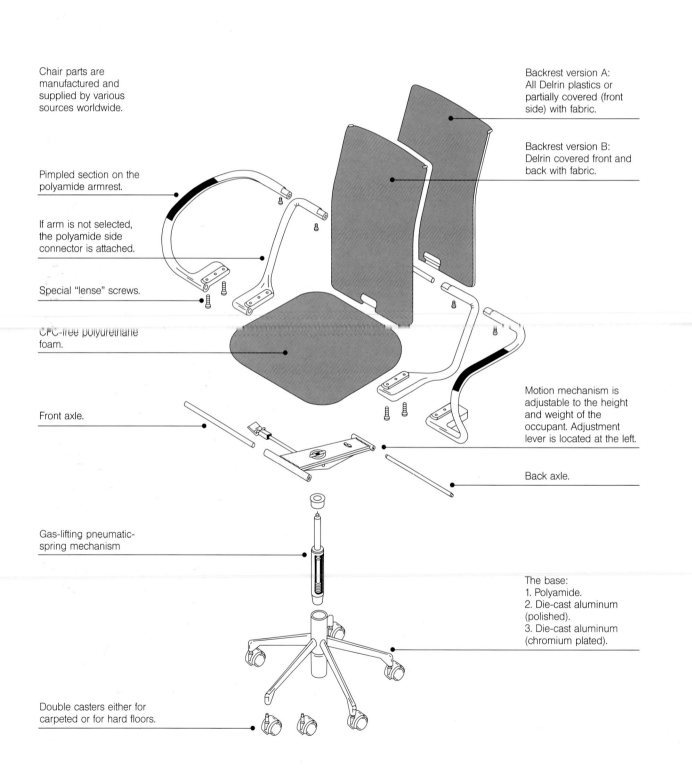

Chair parts are manufactured and supplied by various sources worldwide.

Pimpled section on the polyamide armrest.

If arm is not selected, the polyamide side connector is attached.

Special "lense" screws.

CFC-free polyurethane foam.

Front axle.

Gas-lifting pneumatic-spring mechanism

Double casters either for carpeted or for hard floors.

Backrest version A: All Delrin plastics or partially covered (front side) with fabric.

Backrest version B: Delrin covered front and back with fabric.

Motion mechanism is adjustable to the height and weight of the occupant. Adjustment lever is located at the left.

Back axle.

The base:
1. Polyamide.
2. Die-cast aluminum (polished).
3. Die-cast aluminum (chromium plated).

Sequential documentation illustrates a chair's assembly. The process begins with all the parts for one chair placed in a transport bin (right). The full assembly is performed by one person, who undertakes the quality control and assures that everything works properly.

25

"Miss Trip" side chair

Designer: Philippe Starck (French, b. 1949)
Manufacturer: Kartell S.p.A., Noviglio (MI), Italy
Date of design: 1995

The original of this chair, more sculpturally voluptuous, was intended to be a self-contained unit, eliminating a carton package. Nevertheless, for economy of shipment, the customer purchases the disassembled chair in its own take-away box. The manufacturer, known, up to now, for its exclusive plastics production, is making its first object employing wood. Two-component molding of polypropylene forms the seat where it reaches considerable thickness (about 8mm) in the inner strata.

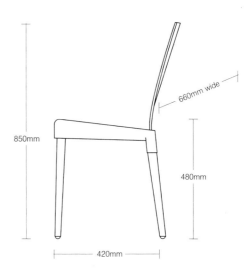

850mm
660mm wide
480mm
420mm

Turned solid beechwood legs are fitted at the top with plastic screws and at the bottom with plastic glides.

Polypropylene seat is molded by a two-component-forming process and includes slits on the back edge for the back's insertion.

The back is bent plywood with a beechwood veneer.

In the original concept (right), the seat and the back served as the packaging container for the legs. The wicker-effect surface was to be part of the mold die. The design was greatly modified in the final production model:

The legs were changed from being force fitted to those with threaded plastic tops which the customer screws into the underside of the seat.

The back was simplified with two slits which fit into the seat and are held by two screws.

The self-contained unit was changed to the chair's being housed in a "cash and carry" cardboard box (450 x 150 x 500mm) (not shown). The assembly-instruction graphics are printed on the outside of the box. The total weight of the box and the chair is 5.5Kg.

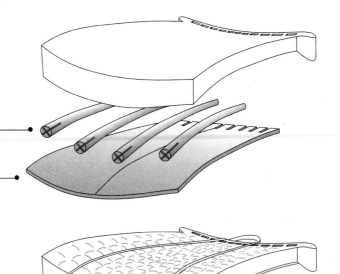

Illustration has been adapted from a sketch by the designer.

26

"Alí-Babá" seat

Designer: Oscar Tusquets Blanca (Spanish, b. 1941)
Manufacturer: Casas M. s.l., Barcelona, Spain
Date of design: 1990

The namesake of the mythical Middle Easterner's
flying carpet, this seat was also inspired by carpets
used on furniture, particularly in British mansions and
by Eliel Saarinen in Finland. On the model where the
carpet-upholstery flows onto the floor, the designer
wanted to create a 2-level design to accommodate
people who watch television or read a newspaper
while sitting on the floor and leaning against a
sofa. The design is made possible by the use of
the flexible polyurethane form housed within the
upholstery bag (carpet on the top, felt on the bottom).

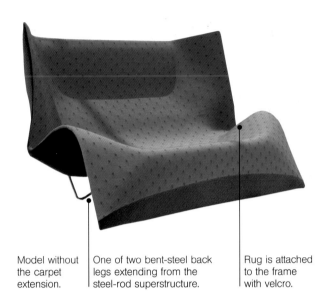

Model without
the carpet
extension.

One of two bent-steel back
legs extending from the
steel-rod superstructure.

Rug is attached
to the frame
with velcro.

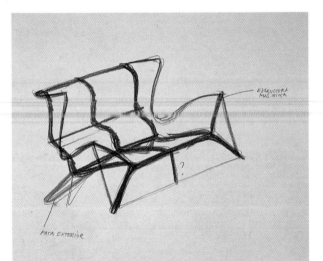

Bent steel superstructure (in the designer's sketch here) is
located inside a flexible polyurethane form which is covered
by the upholstery (carpet on the top, felt underneath).

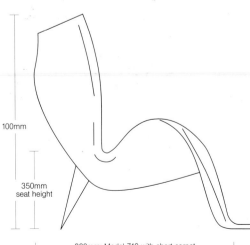

100mm

350mm
seat height

860mm: Model 740 with short carpet

2300mm: Model 740 with extended carpet

Three carpet designs
are available (Tibet,
left; Anatolia, middle;
Laberinto, right). Also,
other fabric or leather
may be used.

AUCHMUTY HIGH SCHOOL
DOVECOT ROAD
GLENROTHES
KY7 5JL

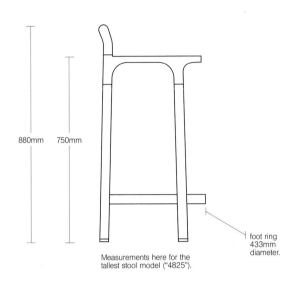

880mm   750mm

foot ring
433mm
diameter.

Measurements here for the
tallest stool model ("4825").

"4822" to "4825" stools

Designer: Anna Castelli Ferrieri (Italian, b. 1920)
Manufacturer: Kartell S.p.A., Noviglio (MI), Italy
Date of design: 1979

Resulting from sophisticated and extensive technological research, this stool was first manufactured in structural polyurethane in order to obtain thick sections and hold the metal insertions in the molding process. However, when the polyurethane was found to have structural limitations, an engineered plastic made of slightly foamed glass-reinforced polypropylene was substituted. The stool has become the manufacturer's biggest selling product at 15,000 annually. The four model numbers refer to varying leg and back heights; otherwise, the stools are the same design.

The test result below of one of the many engineering studies performed on the Castelli Ferrieri seat illustrates where major stress deformation occurs (shown in red).

Expanded polyurethane backrest/handle covers an iron structural rod.

Seat in semi-expanded polypropylene, filled with glass.

Structural iron rod terminates in a threading that accommodates the screwing on of the detachable legs.

Painted iron legs.

Footrest in polypropylene (filled with a metal ring) stiffens the four slim metal legs.

Rubber plugs finish the legs and protect the floor.

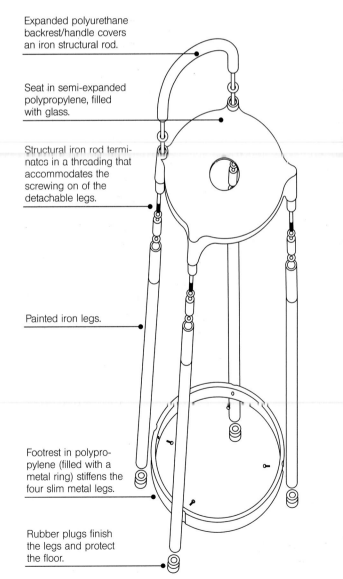

The four stool heights and two backrest/handles are available in a range of models including those below and others: Seven model numbers from "4822" to "4828."

28

"Hi Ho" stool

Designer: Aaron Lown (American, b. 1968)
Manufacturer: Aaron Lown—C4 Design
Laboratories, New York, NY, U.S.A.
Date of design: 1994

Lightweight aluminum for the base, formed
by an age-old sandcasting process, and
the fiberglass shell, shaped in a vacuum
bag, are combined to produce a springy
seat in an unusual shape. The foot pegs
which support the occupant are also used
to hold the stool sections together. Industrial
materials have been combined with a
luxury one—leather.

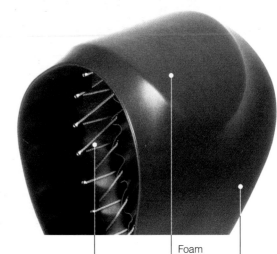

Lacing holds the leather to the fiberglass.

Foam padding beneath the leather.

Leather cover.

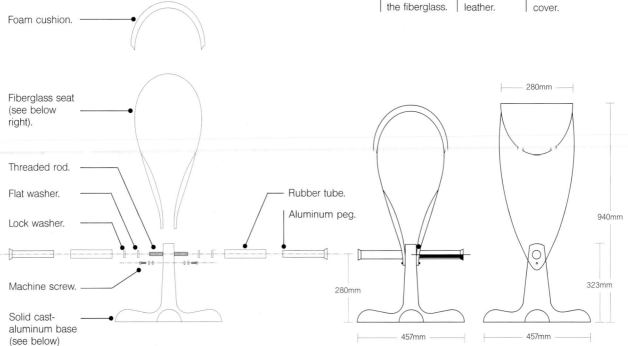

Foam cushion.

Fiberglass seat (see below right).

Threaded rod.

Flat washer.

Lock washer.

Rubber tube.

Aluminum peg.

Machine screw.

Solid cast-aluminum base (see below)

280mm

940mm

323mm

280mm

457mm

457mm

A traditional sand mold casts the solid-
aluminum base, shown here before
casting.

12 layers of medium-weight woven glass and woven roving are placed on a
form (right) and adhered to the form in a plastic vacuum bag. After forming,
the fiberglass section (left) is covered by a leather sleeve and laced beneath.

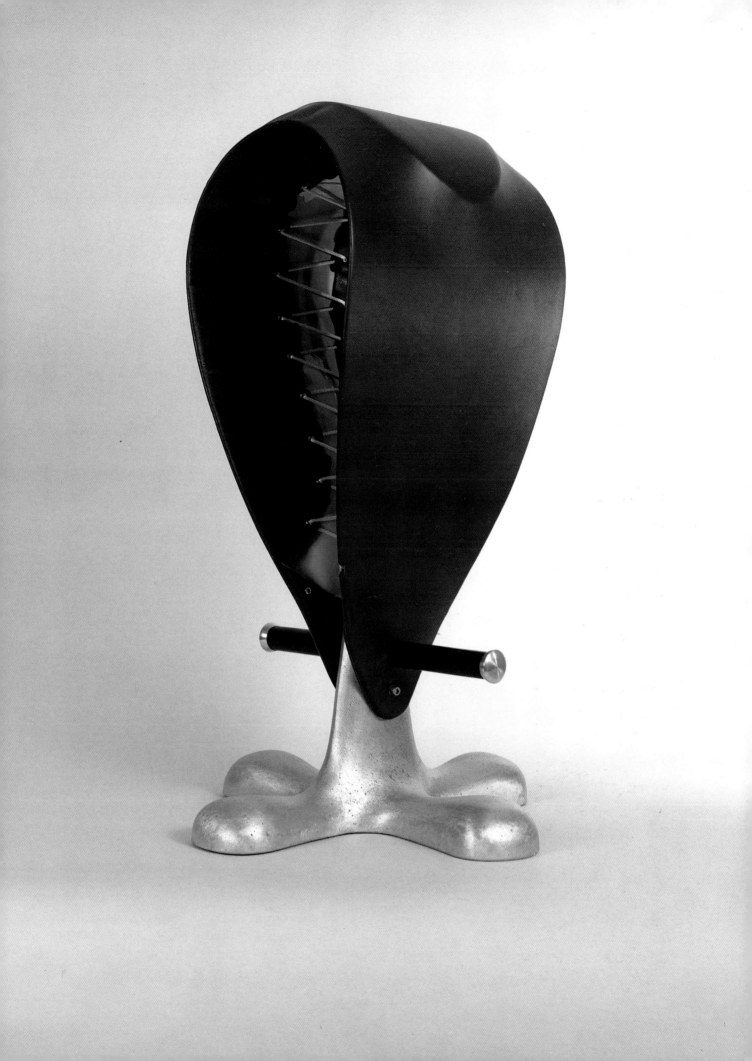

"Pepe" chair

Designer: Christopher Connell (Australian, b. 1955)
and Raoul C. Hogg (New Zealander, b. 1955)
Manufacturer: MAP–Merchants of Australian
Product Pty. Ltd, Victoria, Australia
Date of design: 1992-93

This lithe, sinuous form and intricate construction
was intended by the designers as an exercise "to
do the most difficult thing we could." A lightweight
tubular steel frame is engulfed by polyurethane
foam in a mold. The two sections of the interior
steel support frame are connected by a special
bracket at the waist of the chair (where the back
meets the seat) to offer appreciable springiness to
the back. The 100% wool crêpe upholstery fabric
is available in a range of colors not normally used
for furniture.

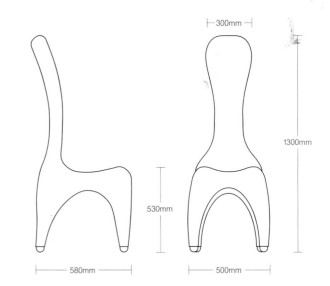

No. 29 continued ▶

29

"Pepe" chair

After the mold is injected with expanded polyurethane foam using a Heko Viking low-pressure foam-dispensing machine, the fully-formed chair with a self-skin is removed with the tubular frame inside.

Bright milled steel tubing (25mm diameter x 1.6mm wall thickness) is bent with a Pedrozzili automatic tube-bending machine and is Saf electric mig welded before being inserted into the mold in an inverted position. The die is then closed and injected with foam.

3-part hinged mold before it is injected with CFC-free expanded polyurethane with the use of a low-pressure foam-dispensing machine.

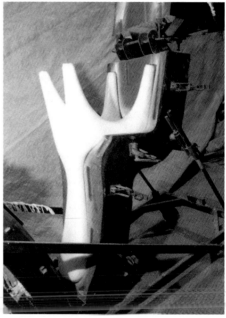

The tubular inner frame is in two parts connected by two hairpin springs which permit the back to flex backward from the seat. (Shown here in the inverted position in which it is molded)

100% wool crêpe upholstery fabric is cut to a pattern and hand sewn onto the self-skinned polyurethane body.

2X hairpin springs connect the two sections of the frame, permitting the back to flex.

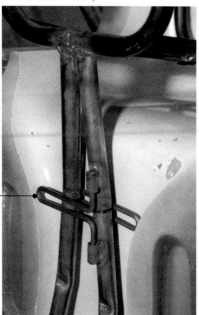
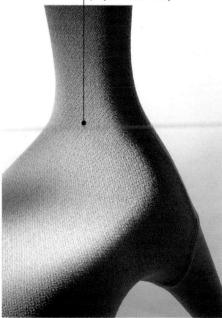

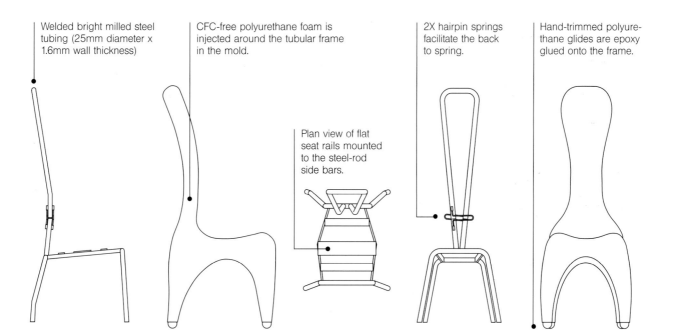

Welded bright milled steel tubing (25mm diameter x 1.6mm wall thickness)

CFC-free polyurethane foam is injected around the tubular frame in the mold.

Plan view of flat seat rails mounted to the steel-rod side bars.

2X hairpin springs facilitate the back to spring.

Hand-trimmed polyure-thane glides are epoxy glued onto the frame.

Workman assembles the "Pepe" chairs in a factory where other chairs are produced.

30

Bubble-wrap chair

Designers: Fernando Campana (Brazilian, b. 1961)
and Humberto Campana (Brazilian, b. 1953)
Manufacturer: Campana Objetos Ltda,
São Paulo/SP, Brazil.
Date of design: 1995

While not exuding permanence, the use of a
material never intended for upholstery suggests
a direction for new fabric development—padding
and upholstery as one and the same material.
The chair was made in an edition of 2.

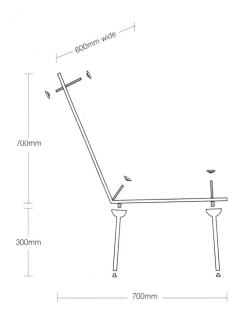

Sheet-metal squares are welded
into the corners of the grid of the
frame. Six bolts which hold down
the bubble wrap are in turn
welded to the metal squares.

5mm diameter
steel rods form a
70 x 70mm grid.

Upholstery: 30 sheets
of bubble wrap
(600 x 1300mm).

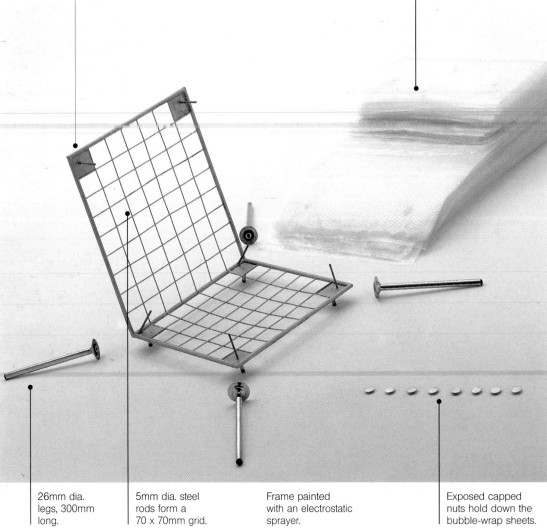

26mm dia.
legs, 300mm
long.

5mm dia. steel
rods form a
70 x 70mm grid.

Frame painted
with an electrostatic
sprayer.

Exposed capped
nuts hold down the
bubble-wrap sheets.

"Sansiro" chair

Designers: Fabrizio Ballardini (Italian, b. 1953)
and Lucio Costanzi (Italian, b. 1957)
Manufacturer: Bernini S.p.A., Carate Brianza
(MI), Italy
Date of design: 1994

This playful, structurally innovative object
questions the boundaries of fine art, seating,
and function. Exploiting the elasticity of
rubber, the seat itself (an inflatable ball) is
essentially a separate object.

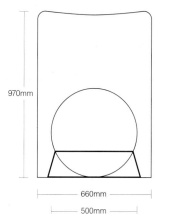
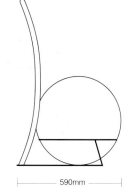

970mm

660mm

500mm

590mm

Rubber glides are
attached to the ends of
the tubular steel
upholstery support.

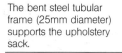

The seating ball (500mm diameter)—formed of two
layers of rubber fused with a non-toxic netting
layer—is spray painted with an emulsion of
metallic fragments and is inflatable by a valve.

The bent steel tubular
frame (25mm diameter)
supports the upholstery
sack.

Metal cross member
holds the hoop frame in
place at the back center.

The solid steel rod frame
(8mm diameter)
supports the ball.

The upholstery sack slides
over the back frame.

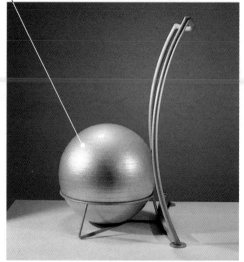

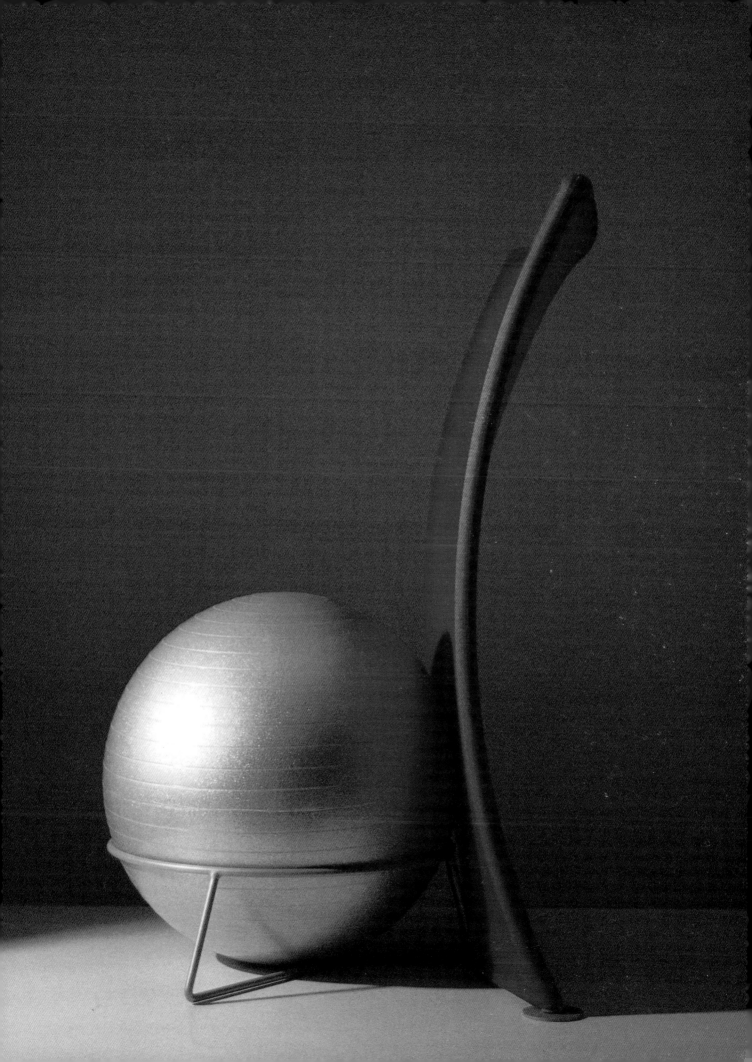

"Lockhead Lounge LC2"

Designer: Marc Newson (Australian, b. 1962)
Manufacturer: Pod, Paris, France
Date of design: 1988

Modified from the original model (the one-of-a-kind "LC1" version), the production of this seat combines a plastic (fiberglass) with a metal (aluminum). The "LC2" is deceptively light in that it weighs only 20Kg due to the hollow fiberglass shell. Designed with only three legs, this unabashed industrial object completely rejects the idea of comfort. It was produced in an edition of 10 and is very expensive.

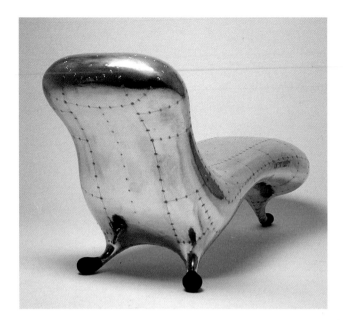

No. 32 continued ▶

"Lockhead Lounge LC2"

Sheets of aluminum are hammered onto the amphoric shape and, like an airplane's body, are riveted onto the fiberglass shell.

The inner shell is formed by fusing sections of fiberglass.

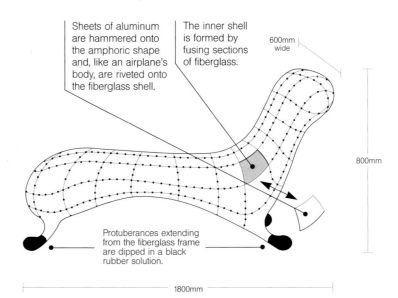

600mm wide

800mm

Protuberances extending from the fiberglass frame are dipped in a black rubber solution.

1800mm

A mold is used for forming the fiberglass shell.

The fiberglass shell is shown here, assembled in one version and, before assembly, in two parts lying on their sides. The back legs are part of the mold; the front leg is attached separately.

A scene from Madonna's music video "Rain" (1992).

The designer and maker is sanding the finished fiberglass form, prior to its being riveted over with aluminum sheets.

"Louis 20" chair

Designer: Philippe Starck (French, b. 1949)
Manufacturer: Vitra GmbH, Weil am Rhein, Germany
Date of design: 1992

Produced with ecological consciousness, this chair consists of two different materials which are recyclable: polypropylene (body and front legs) and already recycled aluminum (back legs and arms). Only five screws are used to connect the back-legs bridge to the body. An optional swiveling writing tablet, attaching to one arm, is available. The energy and raw material required for reprocessing polypropylene is 70% less than that for polyamide. Polypropylene is a thermoplastic with 99% purity, making it an excellent candidate for a raw material with the same characteristics as the original.

Back half of die in the blow molding process.

Chair body is formed when a warm plastic tube is placed within the closed mold and compressed air forces it against the shape of the hot die—a technique known as blow molding.

Chair body before the excess polypropylene is trimmed away from the top, bottom and between the front legs. Available in gray, blue, red, green, black, or blue-gray.

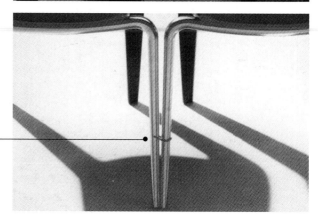

Connecting wire links together back legs for ganging in rows for assembly hall use.

No. 33 continued ▶

"Louis 20" chair

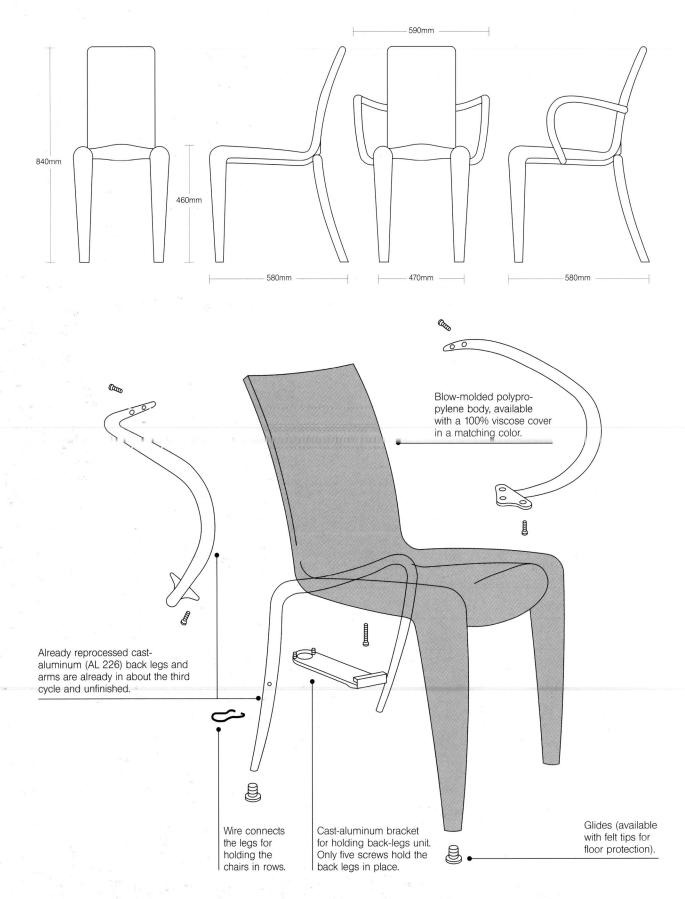

840mm

460mm

590mm

580mm

470mm

580mm

Blow-molded polypro-
pylene body, available
with a 100% viscose cover
in a matching color.

Already reprocessed cast-
aluminum (AL 226) back legs and
arms are already in about the third
cycle and unfinished.

Wire connects
the legs for
holding the
chairs in rows.

Cast-aluminum bracket
for holding back-legs unit.
Only five screws hold the
back legs in place.

Glides (available
with felt tips for
floor protection).

Fibers and Composites

"Light Light" armchair

Designer: Alberto Meda (Italian, b. 1945)
Manufacturer: Alias, Grumello del Monte (BG), Italy
Date of design: 1987

The designer, who began as an engineer more than a quarter of a century ago, has created a chair which reflects his continuing commitment to pursuing fresh, new, technologically innovative approaches to traditional objects. This chair was constructed with a core of Nomex honeycomb which was covered over with carbon fiber, itself saturated with an epoxy resin before application. All of which resulted in the lightest, fully functional chair known, at almost 1Kg.

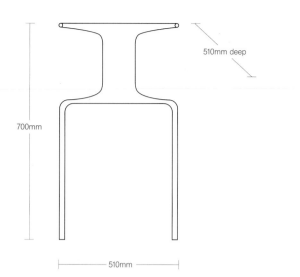

510mm deep

700mm

510mm

Experimental materials used in the early trials of production.

First in yellow polystyrene made by the designer.

A subsequent version in polyurethane.

Parts and pieces of an experimental version weigh in at about 0.75Kg, before the final assembly with adhesives added.

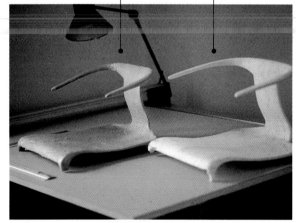

No. 34 continued ▶

"Light Light" armchair

Sandwich configuration is accomplished with a resin mold, "empty sack," and autoclave (or an apparatus, like that for medical sterilization, employing hyperheated steam under pressure).

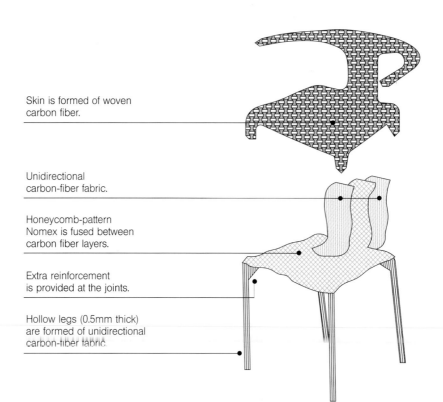

Skin is formed of woven carbon fiber.

Unidirectional carbon-fiber fabric.

Honeycomb-pattern Nomex is fused between carbon fiber layers.

Extra reinforcement is provided at the joints.

Hollow legs (0.5mm thick) are formed of unidirectional carbon-fiber fabric.

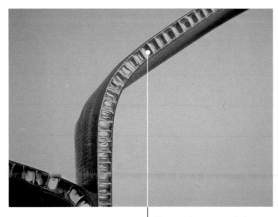

Nomex honeycomb is fused between layers of carbon fiber.

The designer works on a prototype.

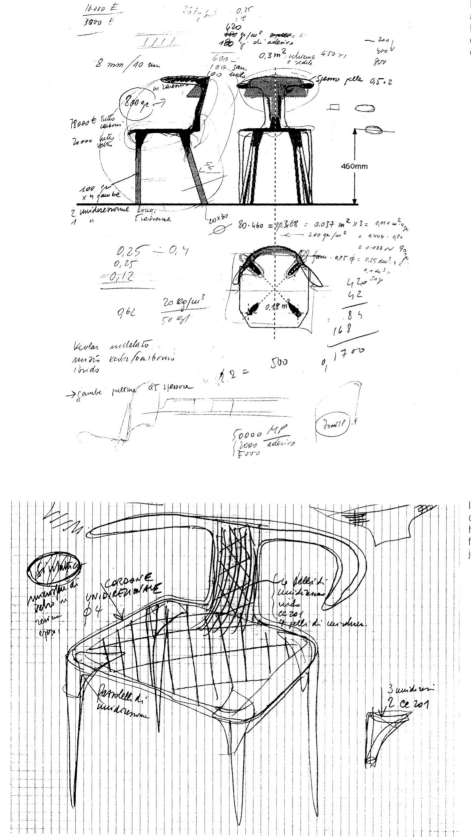

As one of the designer's drawings reveals, his "Light Light" chair was more driven by science than aesthetics, although the latter can never be absent no matter the designer's training or orientation.

In another of the designer's drawings he addresses fiber direction and joint reinforcement.

"Aeron" swivel armchair

Designer: William "Bill" Stumpf (American, b. 1936)
and Don Chadwick (American, b. 1936)
Manufacturer: Herman Miller, Inc., Zeeland,
Michigan, U.S.A.
Date of design: 1992

The result of extensive testing and experimentation
and based on the designers' long experience
in ergonomics, this chair combines many advanced
materials, including die-cast glass, reinforced
polyester, polyurethane foam, flexible vinyl, recycled aluminum, Hytrel polymer, and lycra. Its
main features are a torselastic-spring device and
an unique upholstery pellicle. The manufacturer
unfortunately acquiesced to making the chair also
available in fabric with traditional foam padding.

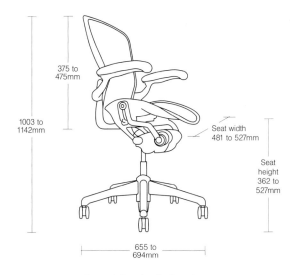

375 to 475mm

1003 to 1142mm

Seat width 481 to 527mm

Seat height 362 to 527mm

655 to 694mm

Range of dimensions for three sizes
(Models A, B, and C)

Protected by numerous patents, the
"Kinemat" tilt feature (an intricate twist
and free-fall tilt action at the ankle and
hip known as torselastic spring)
includes adjustable arms and chair
heights to suit the individual occupant.

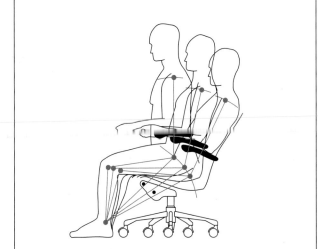

Versions are available in three sizes
(Models A, B, and C) to satisfy the
almost full range of male and female
body sizes, and, democratically, none
is the managerial or secretarial office
chair designs.

No. 35 continued ▶

"Aeron" swivel armchair

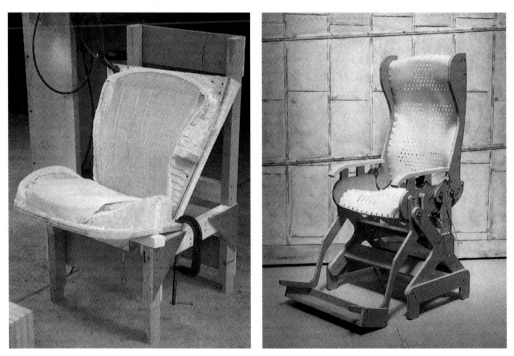

Early test models which eventually resulted in three different sizes to suit the range of human male and female sizes and proportions, up to about 112Kg.

Workman attaches the patented "Kinemat" tilting device, a 4-bar link suspension system.

Exceptional to Vitra's production of the "AC1" chair which is assembled by a single worker (see page 77), Herman Miller assigns different people to assemble this chair.

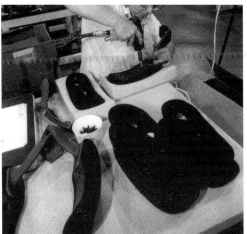

130mm height adjustment
control for the armrest.

Tilt-tension and height
adjustment knobs.

Arm pad supports
(upholstered poly-
urethane foam or non-
upholstered molded
vinyl) and arm yokes
(die-cast aluminum)
offer 30° lateral
rotation.

Anthropo-
morphic
contours.

Developed particularly for this chair, the
pellicle (or upholstery sling) on the back
and the seat is lino-woven from a combi-
nation of lycra and Hytrel elastomeric
polymer. It adapts to the occupant's shape
and becomes typographically neutral
when vacant. The material, which aerates
the body, has been extensively tested for
static load, drop impact, memory, and
abrasion and snag.

Recycled reinforced polyester seat and
back frames.

Self-skinning urethane lumbar pad
(optional) offers 100mm vertical and
25mm horizontal adjustments.

Hip pivots on each side of the seat.

4-bar link suspension system (patented
"Kinemat" tilting device).

152mm-high 2-stage pneumatic (gas) lift.

Recycled cast-aluminum base with a
wrinkle-coated powder-coated epoxy finish.

"Cadé" armchair

Designer: Luciana Martins (Brazilian, b. 1957)
and Gerson de Oliveira (Brazilian, b. 1970)
Manufacturer: Probjeto S.A.–Produtos e Objetos
Projetados, São Paulo, Brazil
Date of design: 1986-87

This unorthodox black cube is not recognizable as a chair. The stretch fabric covering the superstructure yields easily when an occupant sinks onto the seat. The inner structure is far more intricate than one might suspect because, after all, it is hidden from view. *Cadé*, the name of the armchair, is a pun on the Portuguese word *cadé*, meaning, "Where is it?," and *cadeira*, meaning "chair."

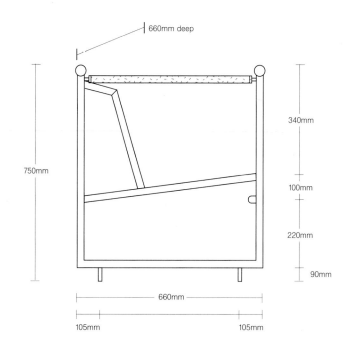

Elastic webbing for the arms and back is attached to the frame with aluminum hooks.

Foam rubber (glued to fabric) is wrapped around the frames of the seat and back.

Steel-tubing frame.

Black epoxy coated superstructure.

Stainless-steel rods for the feet.

The stretch fabric covering is attached to the frame by aluminum hooks attached to the bottom tubes.

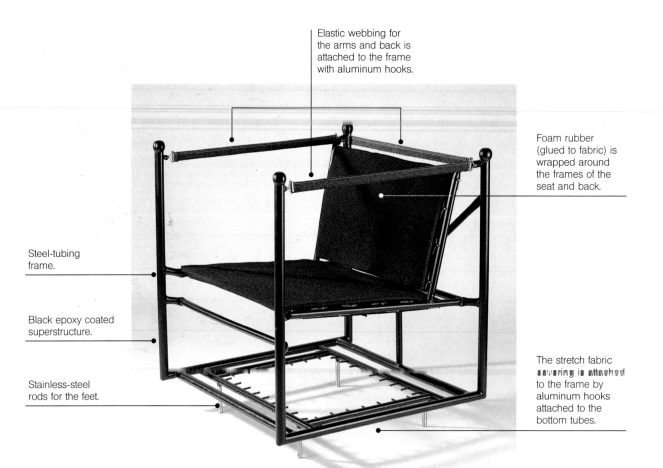

The black stretch-fabric shroud is Elastex (92% nylon and 8% Elastan fiber), manufactured by Char-Lex Indústrias Têxteis.

"Quadraonda" armchair

Designer: Mario Cananzi (Italian, b. 1959)
Manufacturer: Vittorio Bonacina & C. s.n.c.,
Lurago d'Erba (CO), Italy
Date of design: 1991

This is an example of the high-quality vegetal-fiber production for which this particular manufacturer has become well-known. The chair combines a traditional natural material (rattan) and technique (weaving and metal bending) with a modern material (chromium-plated steel) and method (electrical welding).

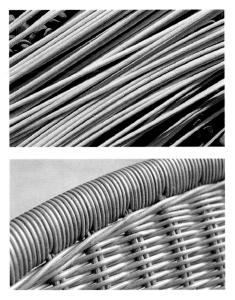

Rattan (a climbing tropical palm) in both the natural state (top) and aniline dyed (below).

A craftsperson weaves the weft (side to side) and warp (top to bottom) arrangement of the rattan reeds onto the bent tubular-steel frame.

With a water-filled steamer, a craftsperson (see hand at extreme right, below) softens the rattan reed to facilitate more malleable weaving onto the metal seat-frame.

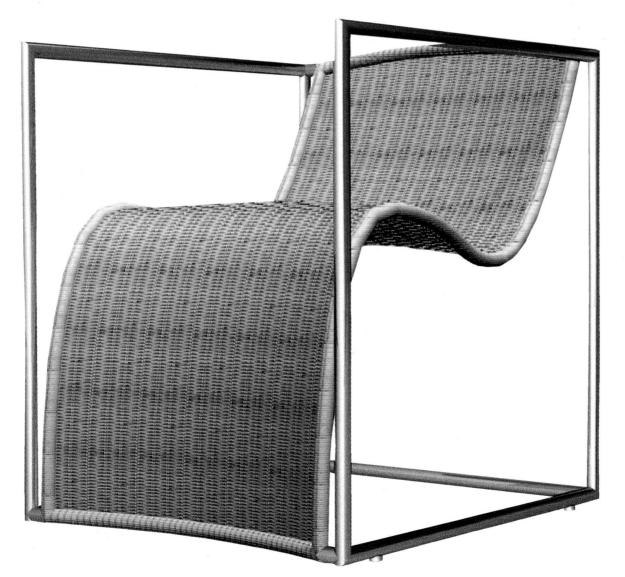

No. 37 continued ▶

37

"Quadraonda" chair

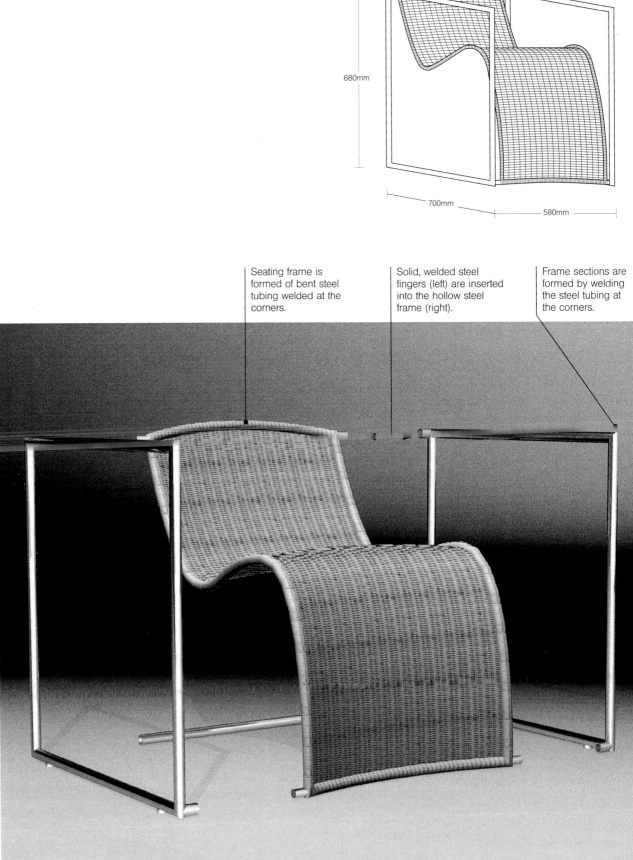

680mm

700mm

580mm

Seating frame is formed of bent steel tubing welded at the corners.

Solid, welded steel fingers (left) are inserted into the hollow steel frame (right).

Frame sections are formed by welding the steel tubing at the corners.

Tubular extensions at the corners of the seat unit are inserted into the welded extensions on the side frames and held by self-threading screws.

An example of the possibility of multiple seating units, or ganging.

"Feltri" armchairs

Designer: Gaetano Pesce (Italian, b. 1939)
Manufacturer: Cassina, Meda (MI), Italy
Date of design: 1986

In a single material that serves as both upholstery and frame while eliminating support bars and other traditional construction elements, this chair was produced from the inextricable relationship among an innovative content, novel techniques, and an unusual material. Felt, a material not normally associated with furniture making, is put to imaginative use. The resin impregnation of the bottom portion creates rigid support, and the pliable quality of the natural felt in the top portion facilitates folding, offering a womb-like space. The design is available in low- and high-back versions.

Back view reveals the folding nature of the intentionally flopped back and arm-wings.

The hemp strings hold the seat to the body.

The circular base is clipped, due to the 25mm thickness of the felt, on the periphery to permit the creation of a smooth curve.

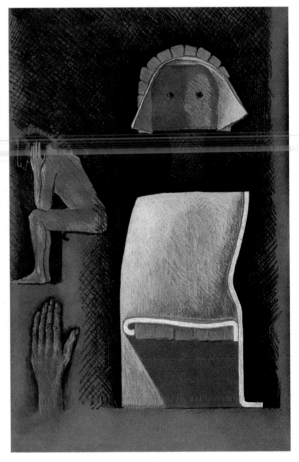

Designer's conceptual drawing (in various media on paper) explores the use of a material which would serve to produce an essentially 2-section chair.

The production model (not shown) by Cassina is fully lined on the inside of the hood with a fabric quilted with polyester wadding.

No. 38 continued ▶

"Feltri" armchairs

Working on a prototype, the felt is impregnated (or soaked) with polyester resin, which when dried under high heat turns the felt into a stiff material, almost like wood.

An inverted prototype chair reveals (in the darker area) the resin-soaked lower portion, beneath the seat.

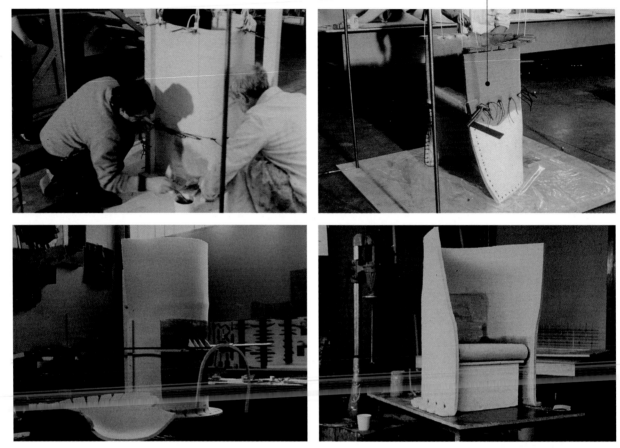

After extensive experimentation, a final production mold is made.

A fully assembled version of the chair with a panel (not used in the final version) added beneath the seat.

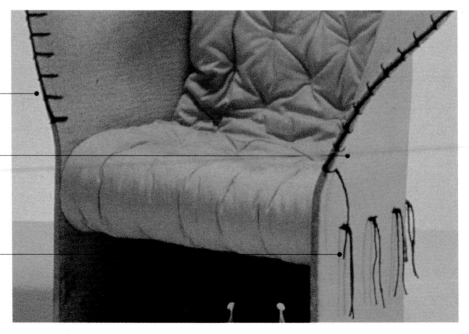

Heavy wool strings are stitched through the periphery to offer binding to the thick edge of the felt and also a finishing touch.

Both the barrel back and the seat are wool felt (25mm thick).

Hemp strings are fed through puncture holes in the side to hold the hard resin-saturated seat in place.

High version, side view.

High version, front view.

Low version, side view, same width and depth as high version.

1300mm

660mm

730mm

450mm

980mm

660mm

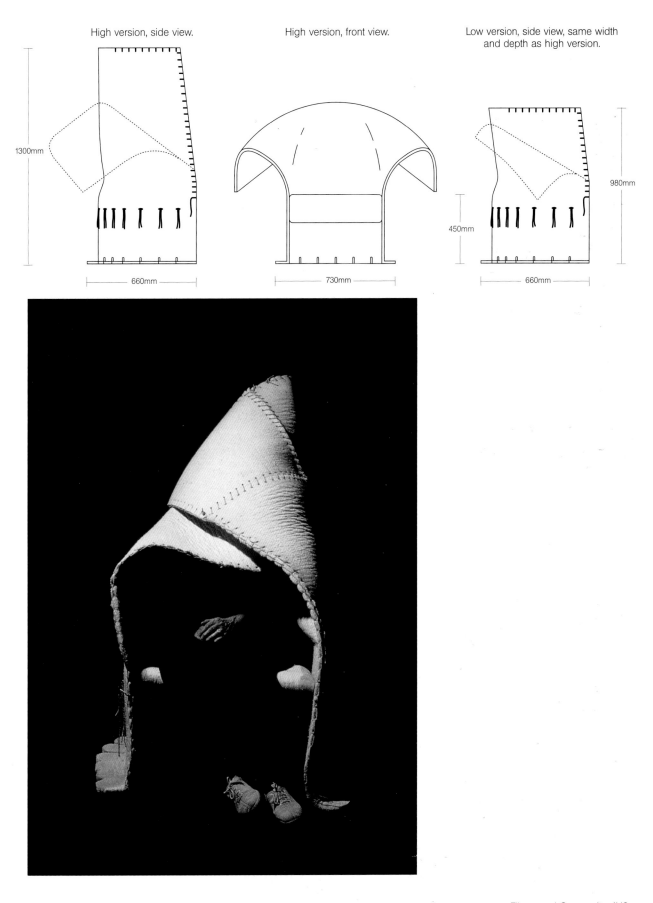

"Knotted" lounge chair

Designer: Marcel Wanders (Dutch, b. 1963)
Manufacturer: Wanders Wonders, Amsterdam,
The Netherlands
Date of design: 1995

Based on the traditional craft of macramé, a rope made of carbon fiber (inside) and an aramid casing (outside sleeve) is knotted into a limp shape, soaked in an epoxy solution, suspended within a frame to form a chair shape, and dried at a high temperature. It becomes very stiff and sturdy. The processes and form were realized through a project known as Dry Tech, sponsored by the Droog Design Foundation in collaboration with the Laboratory for Aeronautics and Astronautics of the T.V. Polytechnic in Delft, The Netherlands. The designer is a member of the ad-hoc Droog Design group; the Dutch word *Droog* means "dry" or possibly "lacking substance."

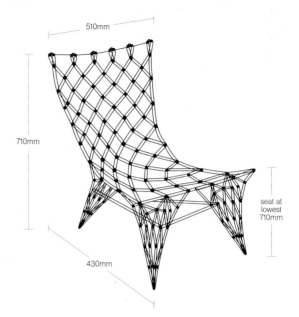

510mm

710mm

430mm

seat at
lowest
710mm

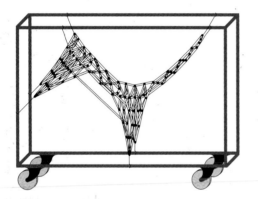

The limp braided chair is saturated in an epoxy solution, hung within a frame in the desired form, and placed in a room heated to 80° C. until the rope (silky carbon fiber covered by a cotton-like, soft aramid sleeve) becomes rigid and extremely strong.

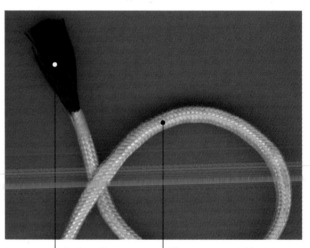

Carbon fibers run inside the length of the aramid sleeve.

The woven aramid sleeve (or bread) (4mm diameter overall) covers the carbon-fiber center.

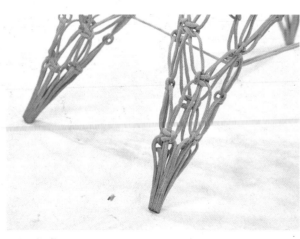

Rigidly formed by an epoxy solution, the legs assume a strong cone shape.

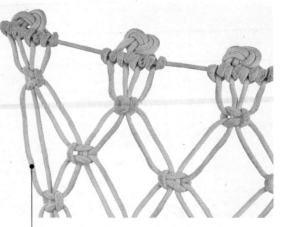

A close view of the top of the back reveals the braided rope, frozen in place as if by magic.

"Husband" armchair

Designer: Constantin Boym
(Russian, b. 1955)
Manufacturer: Boym Design Studio,
New York, New York, U.S.A.
Date of design: 1992

Admired by Philippe Starck and
specified for installation by him in
the Teatríz restaurant in Mexico City,
this chair reflects a nostalgia for a
time past. It features a so-called
"husband" backrest, while
exemplifying a kind of banality
with kitsch values. The chair is
part of a group which the designer
has named Searstyle furniture.

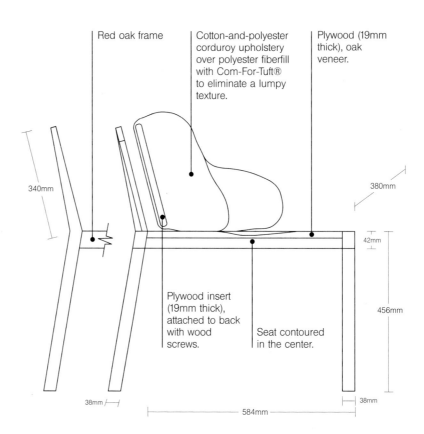

Red oak frame

Cotton-and-polyester
corduroy upholstery
over polyester fiberfill
with Com-For-Tuft®
to eliminate a lumpy
texture.

Plywood (19mm
thick), oak
veneer.

340mm

380mm

42mm

Plywood insert
(19mm thick),
attached to back
with wood
screws.

Seat contoured
in the center.

456mm

38mm

584mm

38mm

The "husband" backrest,
normally used to prop
up oneself in bed, was
ordered directly from the
Sears, Roebuck & Co.
catalogue by the designer.
It is split open in the back,
a plywood panel inserted
(see the drawing above),
and the back resewn
closed.

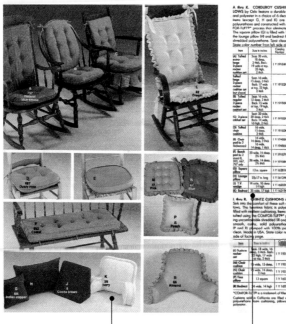

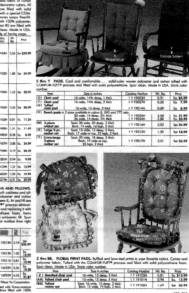

The "husband" is
illustrated in the
Sears, Roebuck
& Co. catalogue,
shown here in
the 1990 edition.

Specifications and
price for the bedrest,
or "husband," appear
on a subsequent
page in the Sears
catalogue.

Publication of the
Sears catalogue
ceased in 1992.

Cotton-string armchair (blue)

Designers: Fernando Campana (Brazilian, b. 1961)
and Humberto Campana (Brazilian, b. 1953)
Manufacturer: Campana Objetos Ltda,
São Paulo/SP, Brazil.
Date of design: 1993

The designers use no preliminary drawings but
rather work direct. Far more formally constructed
than it appears in its completed form, the metal-
grid body is composed of precisely welded steel
rods which form a screened volume. The cotton
cord is wound through the cage, like a worm
traveling through soil, until a sufficiently cush-
ioned web is woven. The chair was made in an
edition of 5.

Brightly dyed cotton cord (2000mm long x 10mm diameter).

The upholstery is created by the matting that occurs when a length
of cotton cord is fed over, under, and through the grid of the body.

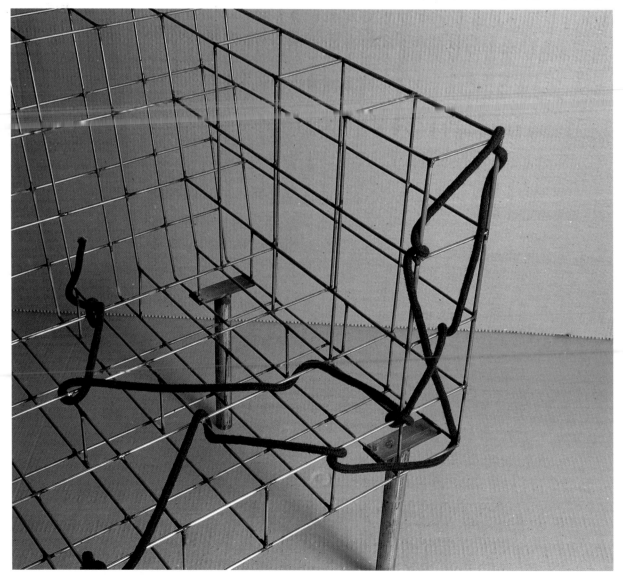

No. 41 continued ▶

41

Cotton-string armchair (blue)

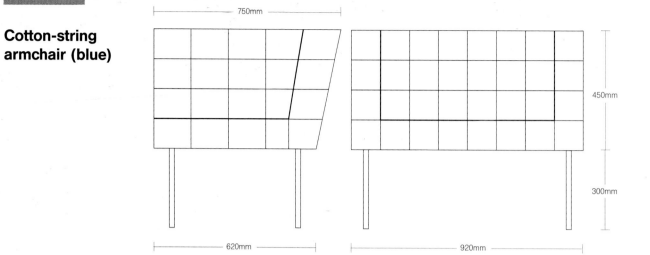

750mm

620mm

450mm

300mm

920mm

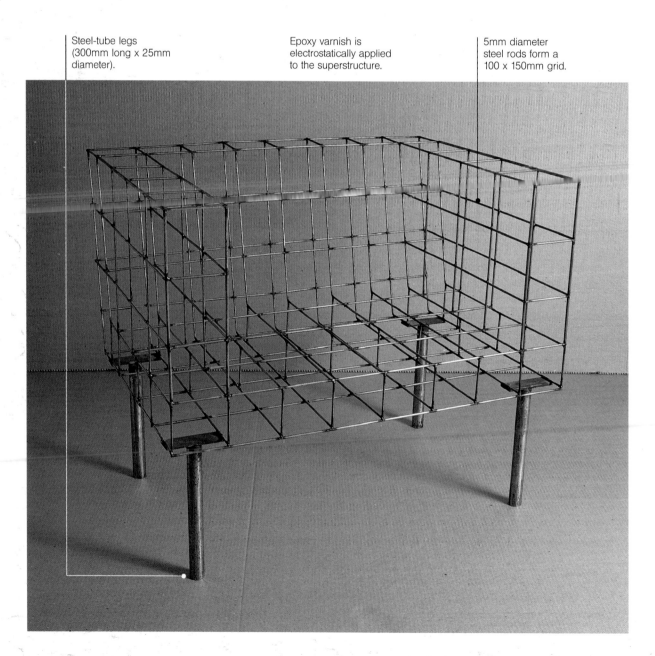

Steel-tube legs
(300mm long x 25mm
diameter).

Epoxy varnish is
electrostatically applied
to the superstructure.

5mm diameter
steel rods form a
100 x 150mm grid.

Various Materials

"Rothko" armchair

Designer: Alberto Liévore (Argentine, b. 1948)
Manufacturer: Indartu, Hernani (Guipúzcoa),
Spain
Dates of design: 1993 (plywood version),
1994 (Maderón version).

The final version of the chair was produced
from high-density Maderón, a proprietary plastic
composite material with wood-like characteristics
which is formed by mixing ground almond
shells and other lingnocellulosic materials with
natural resins and formed by molding. Maderón,
invented by chemical engineer Silio Cardona,
is waterproof and can be made heat resistant.
(Spain, the place of the chair's manufacture
and design, is the second largest harvester
of almonds worldwide; the U.S.A. is the first.)

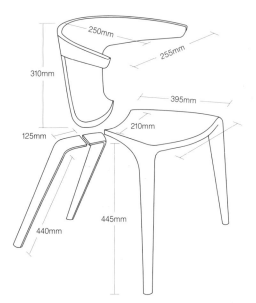

The first version (1993) of the chair
in four sections of 11 mm-thick plywood.

The original plywood prototype evolved
from the 4-section model (above) to the
final Maderón molded version (below).

Due to the high-density nature of the
composite, a very smooth surface is
achievable through sanding.

The ledge on the back frame is glued
and screwed to the underside of the
front section.

After assembly, "C" clamps hold the back
section to the front section until the glue
dries.

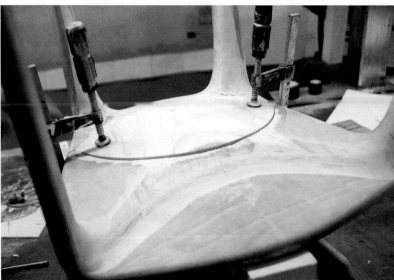

No.42 continued ▶

42

"Rothko" armchair

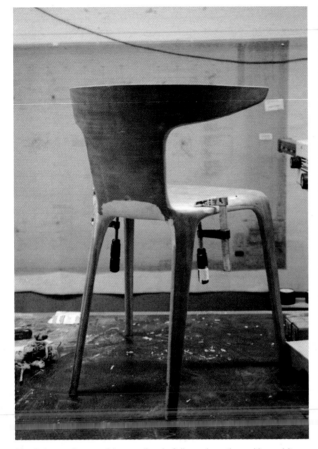

Final stage of assembly, sanding is followed coating with a white varnish and then painting.

The chair installed in its namesake, the Rothko bar in Barcelona.

Almonds used in the production of Maderón before the shells are pulverized.

Production process of Maderón:

Pulverized almond shells
or other lingnocellulosic refuse

+

polymer resins

=

pacto molded
into sections

=

two sections adhered
to each other with epoxy glue

=

assembly is sanded,
painted with white varnish,
and then painted over
with the final varnish color.

The designer was commissioned to
design a chair for the new Rothko bar in
Barcelona. His preliminary ideas (above)
were derived from the traditional Spanish
bar chair (right) originally produced in
bentwood, which for the Rothko chair
proved to be too expensive. The use of
molded Maderón reduced costs by 50%.

"Equity" armchair

Designer: J.-H. Pollard (French, b. 1952)
Manufacturer: Matteograssi S.p.A.,
Mariano Comense (CO), Italy
Date of design: 1987

Employing traditional leather with a
plastic inner layer stiffener, this luxurious
architectonic essay has a presence that
cannot easily be ignored and solves the
problem of shipping a very large object.

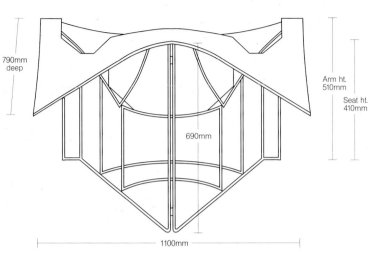

View of the chair from behind.

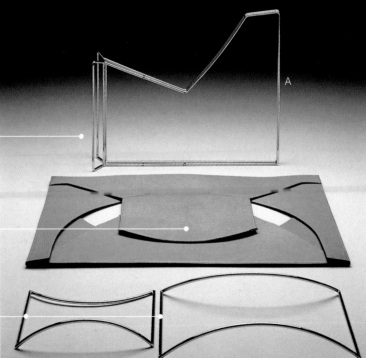

Leather and polyamide-film seat.

Seat support rests on the frame.

Tubular-steel stiffeners for the leather support.

The tubular steel elements are made
available either polished, chromium
plated, spray painted with a metallized
emulsion, or liquid laminated with two
layers of Softech™ (a baked-on finish in
an 80–120 micron thickness).

Serving as legs, the frame folds out from
a central point (A) and serves as the
back, arm, and seat support.

Folded one-piece upholstery:
two layers of coated leather (black or
tan) are fused with an inner layer of
polyamide film. Different thicknesses of
polyamide are inserted in various areas,
depending on the stiffness required.

Inner supports for the seat area (front
edge, right; back side, left) that appear
as arcs on the floor.

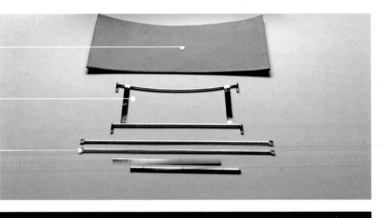

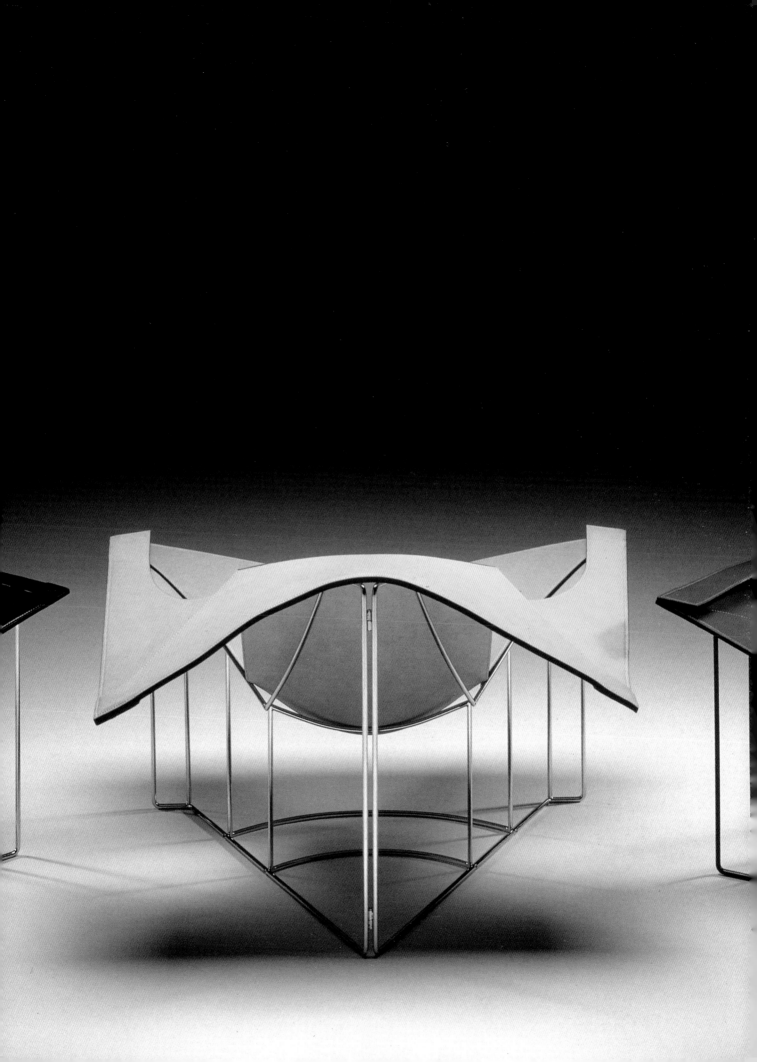

44

"T. 4. 1." (Tea for One) armchair

Designer: Olivier Leblois (French, b. 1947)
Manufacturer: Quart de Poil', Paris, France
Date of design: 1995

This two-part cardboard armchair, supporting
the weight of an adult, may be used for both
domestic and public applications, including with
imprinted advertising messages or art images.
Inexpensively shippable, the chair is sold flat.
Surprisingly, most retail buyers have been those
desiring a kind of throw-away, cheap aesthetic
rather than an utilitarian, inexpensive object
(about 150F./\$30/£20). Compare this chair
with the 1967 example by Claude Courtecuisse
(*Dictionnaire International des Arts Appliqués
et du Design*, Paris: Éditions du Regard, 1996).

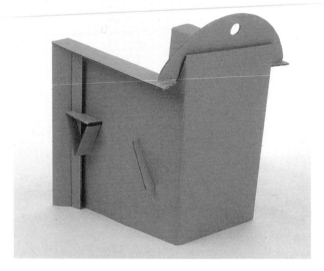

The first edition of the chair (in 3-ply cardboard,
twice as heavy as 2-ply) was stamped out with
blades extended from a flat wooden bed. The
second and present edition (in 2-ply cardboard, shown
here as a simplified interpretation) is cut out by blades
inset into a wooden drum which rolls over flat sheets
of cardboard, like a printing press, rapidly stamping
out each of the two sections.

The interpretation here, for graphic purposes, is
not technically accurate.

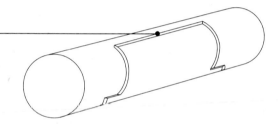

Back and seat
section →

(Broken lines
indicate folds.)

| 340mm | 180mm | 150mm | 150mm | 420mm | 415mm |

550mm
540mm

Cut-outs.

360mm

Sides, arms,
and back-support
and arms section →

610mm

Cut-outs.

20mm 750mm 750mm 20mm

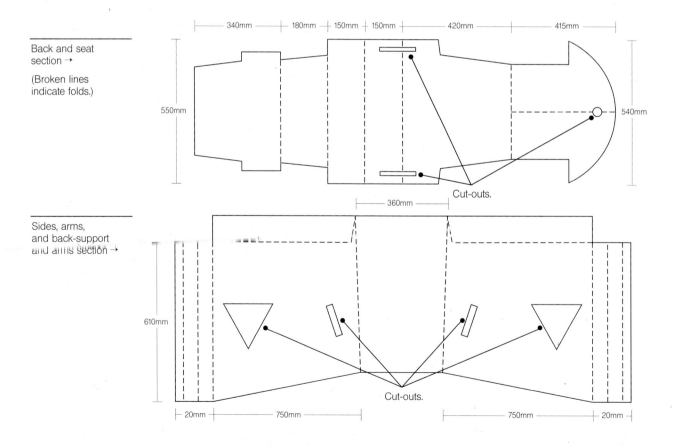

45

"Collezione Pak" armchair

Designer: Nani Prina (Italian, b. 1938)
Manufacturer: Rimadesio S.p.A.,
Desio (MI), Italy
Date of design: 1984

Reminiscent of De Stijl principles, a simple interpretation marries two traditional materials—glass and wood—creating an object far less fragile than it may appear. The glass and wood never touch due to the use of an advanced special adhesive (made of acrylic resins) for connecting the black steel cylinders that separate the glass from the painted wood. The color range includes combinations of black, white, red, yellow-green, and blue.

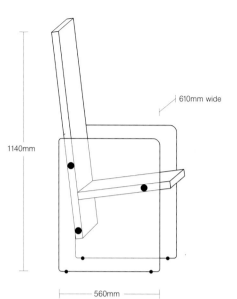

610mm wide

1140mm

560mm

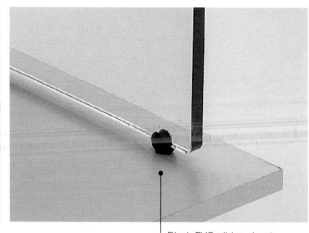

Black steel joints separate the inner glass surface from the back and seat units. They are screwed into the wood and welded to the glass with a special glue (made of acrylic resins) through polymerization with black-light blue lamps—similar to the bonding techniques used in dental ceramics.

15mm thick tempered glass with rounded corners and polished edges.

The wood seat and back surfaces are lacquered.

Black PVC glides elevate the glass edge from the floor for protection.

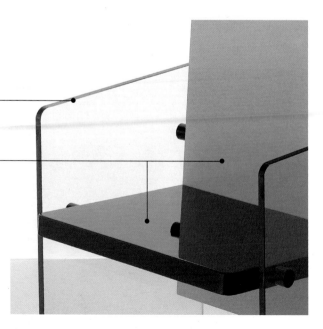

"Ghost" armchair

Designers: Cini Boeri Mariani (Italian,
b. 1924) and Tomu Katayanagi (Japanese,
b. 1950)
Manufacturer: Fiam Italia S.p.A., Tavullia
(PS), Italy
Date of design: 1987

Reforming the reputation of glass as
an overly fragile material, the chair is
one piece and bent in a furnace. The
technique was developed by Antonio
Livi, who in 1972 founded Fiam, the
manufacturer that has since produced
a wide range of deftly twisted and
turned glass furniture.

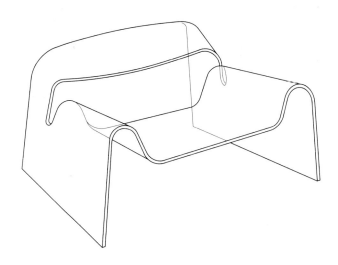

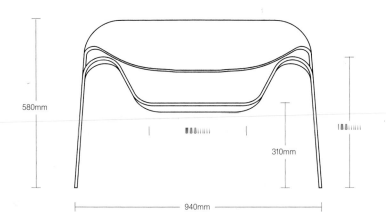

580mm

310mm

940mm

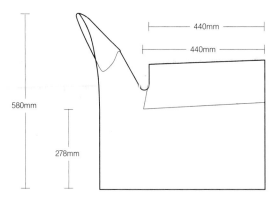

440mm

440mm

580mm

278mm

630mm

"Ghost" armchair

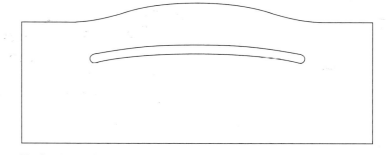

The flat shape of pre-cut float crystal (12mm thick) is shown here before bending occurs. The pierced section within accommodates the upward bending of the bottom of the backrest and the downward bending of the back of the seat.

Float crystal is warm bent in a tunnel furnace, using an exclusive process developed by Antonio Livi at Fiam Italia.

Articulation

"Dafne" folding chair

Designer: Gastone Rinaldi (Italian, b. 1920)
Manufacturer: Fly Line S.r.l., Carrè (VI), Italy
Date of design: 1979

Economical and highly portable, about 180,000 examples of this chair have been produced during the last 15 years. An array of mechanical and hydraulic presses and cutting, bending, and drilling machines are used for the production of the parts which are manually assembled. The chair is available in 10 colors.

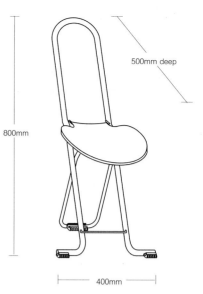

500mm deep

800mm

400mm

The range of colors available.

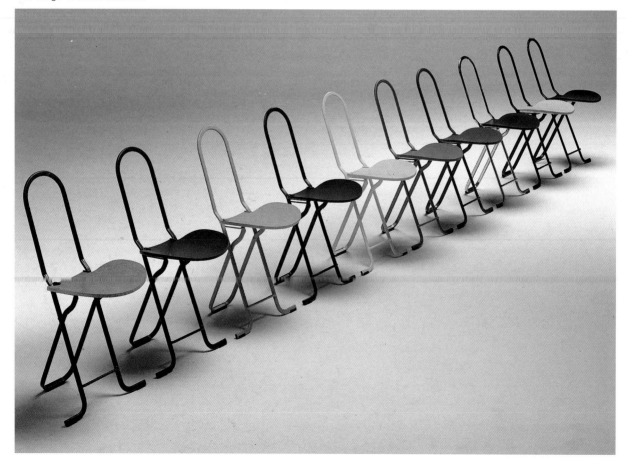

No.47 continued ▶

"Dafne" folding chair

In addition to fine-wood laminated composition board, a version of the chair is available with the seat frame woven over with wicker (straw), a technique still today combined with high-tech designs in Italy.

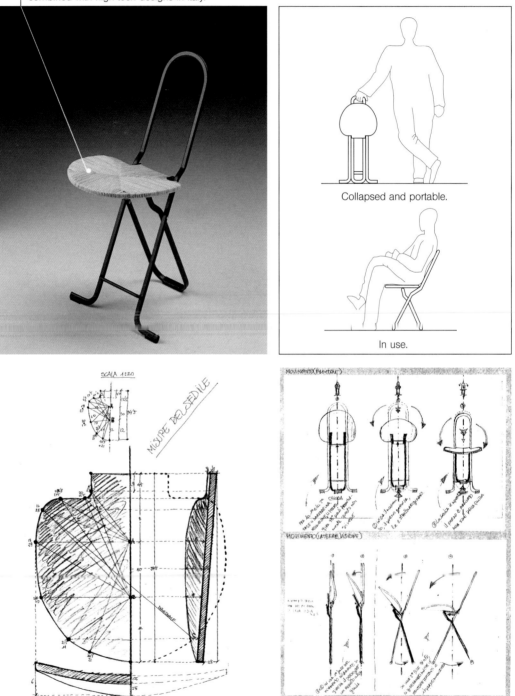

Collapsed and portable.

In use.

Even though the concept is a simple one, the designer performed extensive experimentation and exploration, illustrated here by three of the numerous drawings—the seat geometry (left) and the folding principle (right).

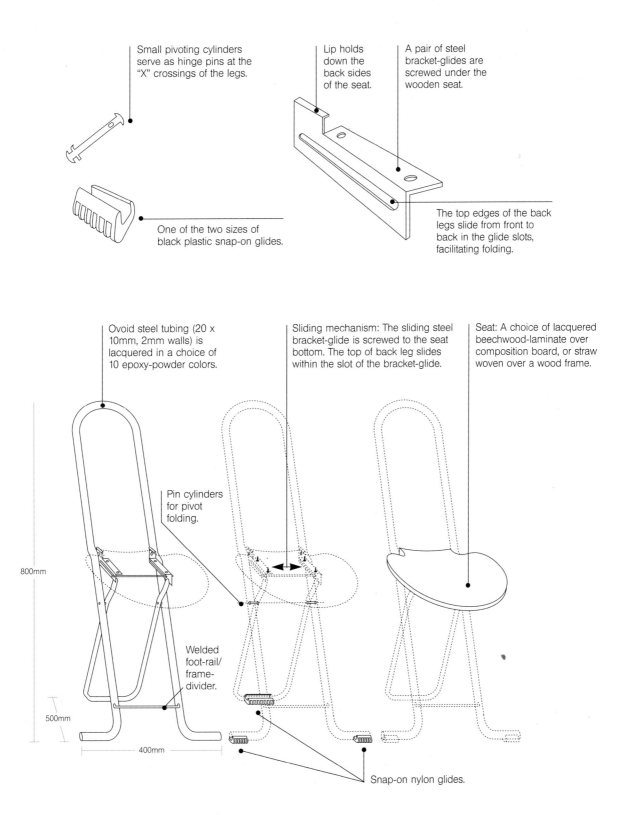

Small pivoting cylinders serve as hinge pins at the "X" crossings of the legs.

One of the two sizes of black plastic snap-on glides.

Lip holds down the back sides of the seat.

A pair of steel bracket-glides are screwed under the wooden seat.

The top edges of the back legs slide from front to back in the glide slots, facilitating folding.

Ovoid steel tubing (20 x 10mm, 2mm walls) is lacquered in a choice of 10 epoxy-powder colors.

Sliding mechanism: The sliding steel bracket-glide is screwed to the seat bottom. The top of back leg slides within the slot of the bracket-glide.

Seat: A choice of lacquered beechwood-laminate over composition board, or straw woven over a wood frame.

Pin cylinders for pivot folding.

Welded foot-rail/frame-divider.

800mm

500mm

400mm

Snap-on nylon glides.

"Rocking–chaîne 1 and 2" chairs

Designer: Jean-Marc Mouligne (French, b. 1950)
Manufacturer: Quart de Poil', Paris, France
Date of design: 1992

Probably more comfortable than it appears, the chairs provide a new definition of the traditional concept of the rocking chair. Easily demountable, these chairs are conveniently shipped and may be used indoors or outside. They are available in zinc and black colors.

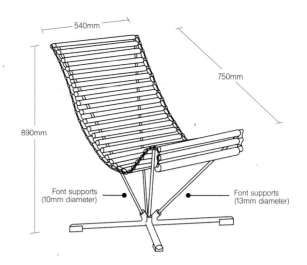

Font supports (10mm diameter)

Font supports (13mm diameter)

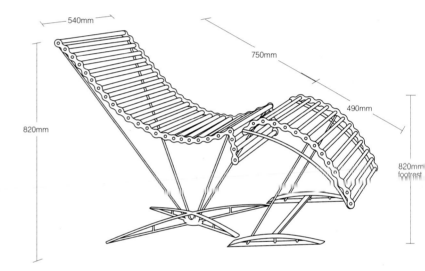

The angle and slope of the seat is adjustable by five notches on the front edge.

The sides are flexing steel joints, much like a bicycle chain or those on a combine harvester.

Polyvinyl glides are attached with two screws.

The cross members are neoprene rubber tubes inserted with full-width stainless steel springs, screwed into the flexing sides.

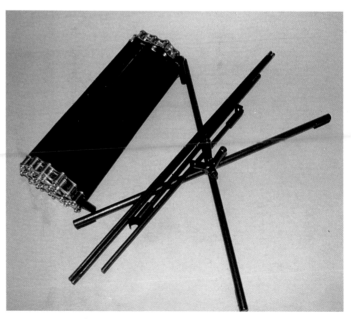

Demountable, all parts of the chairs are assembled without screws or glue. The weight of the chair and occupant holds the parts together.

"Snap" chair

Designer: Peter Costello (Australian, b. 1947)
Manufacturer: Pongrass Furniture Pty. Ltd, Sydney,
Australia
Date of design: 1992

Very precise geometry was required in the production of this chair in order to make the folding
function operate properly and remain closed when
folded. When open the chair is a taut and rigid
unit. It has been extensively tested by the Australian
Furniture Research and Development Institute.
The use of marine plywood and stainless-steel
hardware and cables reveals the designer's
experience as a boat builder.

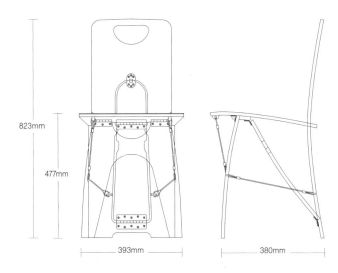

The parts of the chair in wood are cut out with a CNC router.
The surface is sprayed finished with a nitro-cellulose lacquer.

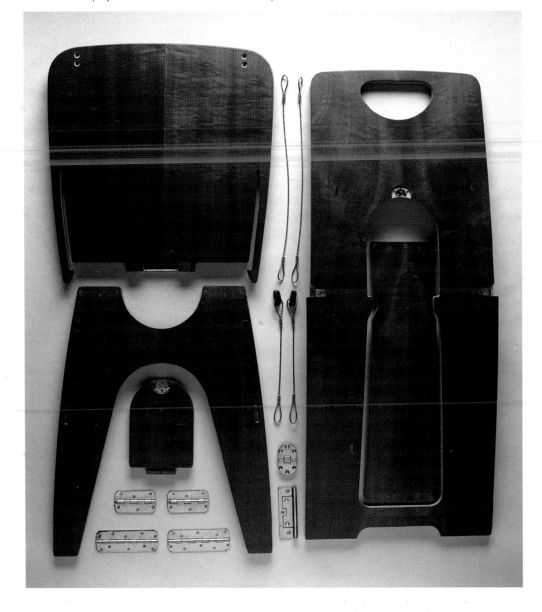

No. 49 continued ▶

49

"Snap" chair

Back right edge of the back support and seat.

Back left leg view of the 2mm stainless-steel cable and crimper.

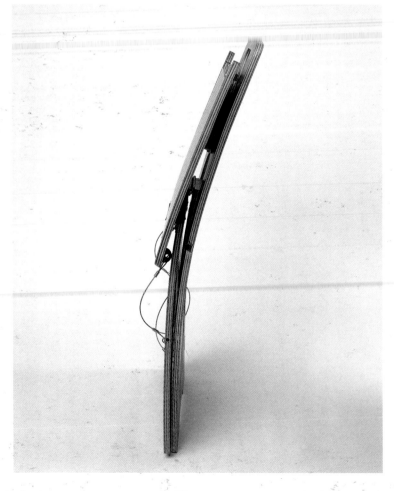

Fully folded, hand-assembled chair.

Electronics

"Body Sonic" seat

Designers: Interior Team, Design Department,
Mazda Motor Corporation
Manufacturer: Mazda Motor Corporation,
Hiroshima, Japan
Date of design: 1989

The most intriguing feature of the seat for the
Mazda MX-5 "Miata" sports car is not the head
pillow that is fitted with sound speakers located
near the occupant's ears. Buried within the body
of the upholstery near the occupant's lumbar
region, there is a vibrating frame device,
connected to the sound system, which assists
in creating a complete body experience of
the sound broadcasted from the dashboard
amplifier.

Pairs of speakers are located
inside each of the front-seat
headrests.

The sound provided by a pair
of speakers and the vibrating
unit housed within the seat is
further augmented by two
woofers (for the bass notes)
and two tweeters (for the high
notes) located in each door.

No. 50 continued ▶

"Body Sonic" seat

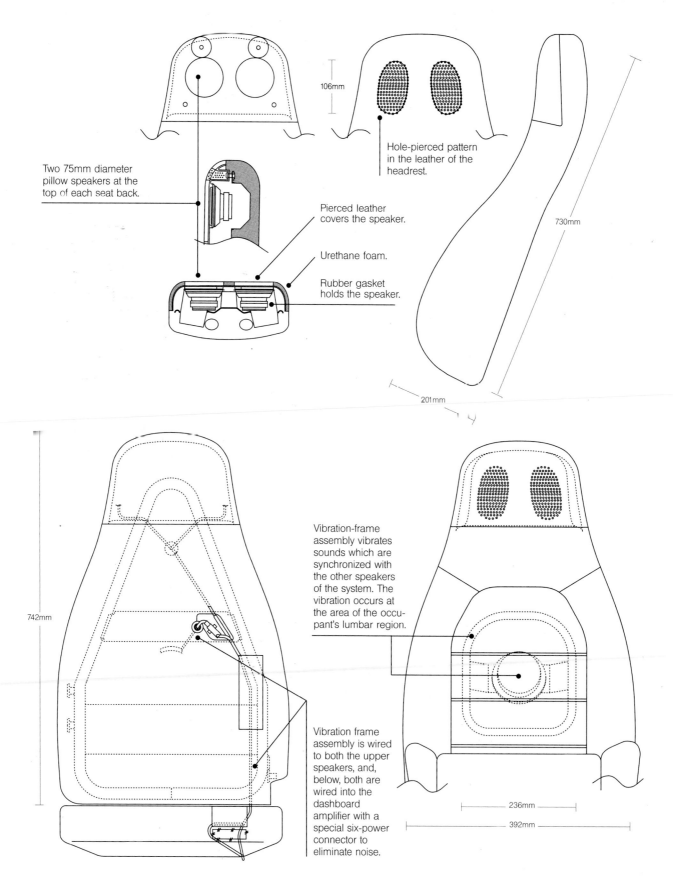

Two 75mm diameter pillow speakers at the top of each seat back.

Pierced leather covers the speaker.

Urethane foam.

Rubber gasket holds the speaker.

106mm

Hole-pierced pattern in the leather of the headrest.

730mm

201mm

742mm

Vibration-frame assembly vibrates sounds which are synchronized with the other speakers of the system. The vibration occurs at the area of the occupant's lumbar region.

Vibration frame assembly is wired to both the upper speakers, and, below, both are wired into the dashboard amplifier with a special six-power connector to eliminate noise.

236mm

392mm

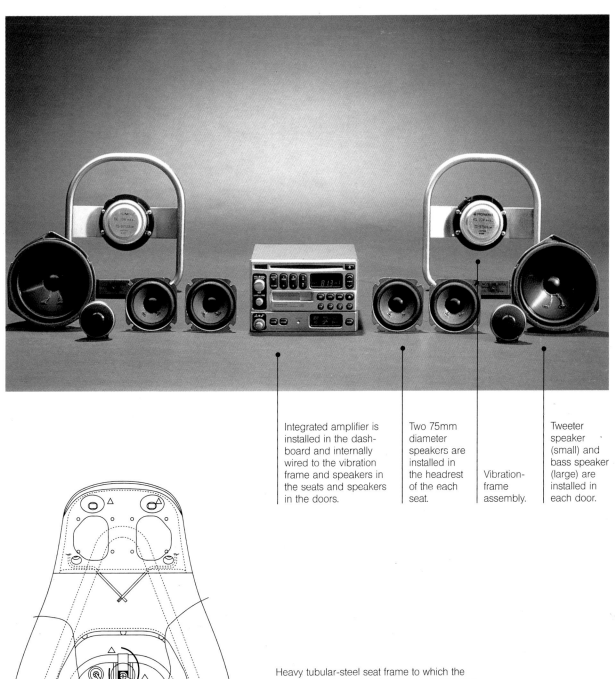

Integrated amplifier is installed in the dashboard and internally wired to the vibration frame and speakers in the seats and speakers in the doors.

Two 75mm diameter speakers are installed in the headrest of the each seat.

Vibration-frame assembly.

Tweeter speaker (small) and bass speaker (large) are installed in each door.

Heavy tubular-steel seat frame to which the speakers and the vibration frame are attached.

Outer ring of the vibration-frame assembly is suspended from the tubular-steel seat frame with rubber bands in three areas.

Indices

Designers

Arad, Ron 50-51
Arosio, Pietro 36-37
Ballardini, Fabrizio 92-93
Boeri, Cini 138-140
Boym, Constantin 122-123
Campana, Fernando & Humberto 48-49,
  90-91, 124-126
Cananzi, Mario 112-115
Costanzi, Lucio 92-93
Castelli Ferrieri, Anna 82-83
Chadwick, Don 106-109
Connell, Christopher 86-89
Costello, Peter 148-150
Davis, James 18-19
Dubuisson, Sylvain 56-57
Eek, Piet Hein 52-55
Essaime (Stéphane Millet) 16-17
Favetta, Maurizio 44-47
Ferreri, Marco 26-29
Forcolini, Carlo 38-39
Gehry, Frank 22-25
Hogg, Raoul C. 86-89
Karpf, Peter 30-32
Katayanagi, Tomu 138-140
Kawecki, David 12-13
Kuramata, Shiro 42-43
Leblois, Olivier 134-135
Liévore, Alberto 128-131
Lown, Aaron 84-85
Lucci, Roberto 68-71
Martins, Luciana 110-111
Mazda Design Department 152-155
Meda, Alberto 64-66, 102-105
Millet, Stéphane 16-17
Morozzi, Massimo 14-15
Mouligne, Jean-Marc 146-147
Newson, Marc 94-97
Ohl, Herbert & Jutta 68-69
Oliveira, Gerson de 110-111
Orlandini, Paolo 68-71
Pesce, Gaetano 116-119
Pollard, J.-H. 132-133
Povey, Stephen 40-41
Prina, Nani 136-137
Rinaldi, Gastone 142-145
Rizzatto, Paulo 60-63
Ruijgrok, Nob 52-55
Schmid, Herbert 20-21
Šípek, Bořek 34-35
Starck, Philippe 78-79, 98-100
Steinmann, Peter 20-21
Stumpf, William 106-109
Tusquets Blanca, Oscar 80-81
Van Praet, Frans 72-73
Walley, David 18-19
Wanders, Marcel 120-121

Manufacturers

Alias S.r.l. 38-39, 64-65, 102-105
Atelier Alinea 20-21
Bernini 92-93
Boym Design Studio 122-123
C4 Design Laboratories 84-85
Casas M. s.l. 80-81
Campana Objetos 48-49, 90-91, 124-126
Cassina 60-63, 116-119
BPA International 26-29
Bonacina, Vittorio, & C. s.n.c. 112-115
Eek & Ruijgrok 52-55
Fiam Italia S.p.A. 138-140
Fly Line 142-145
Herman Miller Furniture Company 106-109
Indartu 128-131
Inredningsform 30-32
Kartell 78-79, 82-83
King Size by Lasar 44-47
Knoll Studio Group 22-25
L.C.S.D. 56-57
MAP—Merchants of Australia Product 86-89
Matrix, divisione della Giorgetti 14-15
Matteograssi 68-69, 132-133
Mazda Motor Corporation 152-155
Metcator-Orteliushuis 72-73
Pod 94-97
Pongrass Furniture 148-150
Probjeto S.A.—Produtos e Objetos
  Projetados 110-111
Quart de Poil' 16-17, 134-135, 146-147
Rimadesio S.p.A. 136-137
Shelby Williams Industries 68-71
Swedese 30-32
3D: Interiors 12-13
Vitra GmbH 34-35, 42-43, 50-51, 98-100
Wanders Wonders 120-121
Yellow Diva 18-19
Zanotta S.p.A. 36-37

General Index

acrylic 46-47
acrylic resin 136
almonds, almond shells 128-130
aluminum 36, 44, 46-47, 52, 54, 56, 58, 63,
  65-66, 76, 84, 94-97, 98, 100, 106-110
amplifier 152, 154-155
aniline dye 14, 112
Antonelli, Paola 9
aramid 120
arc welding 40
Arts and Crafts tradition 9
ashwood 34
autoclave 104
basket, bushel 22
beechwood 14, 16, 20, 26, 78, 145
bentwood 16, 20, 22
birchwood 12
black-light blue lamp 134
blow molding 98
Breuer, Marcel 36
bubble wrap 90
"C" clamps 128
Calder, Alexander 38
Campana brothers 10
carbon fiber 102, 104, 120
cardboard 134
Cardona, Silio 128
carpet-upholstery 80
casters 70, 76, 106-109
ceramics 136
CFC (chloroflourocarbon) 76, 88-89
Char-Lex Indústrias Têxteis 110
chromium 20, 76, 112, 132
CNC router 148
computer 11-12, 50, 52, 54
concrete/polyester 72
copper 34
cotton 122
cotton cord 124
dacron 18
Dal Fabbro, Mario 7
De Stijl 134
Deganello, Paolo 74
Delrin 74, 76
dental ceramics 136
"Documenta" chair 74
Domus 9
Droog Design Foundation 120
Droog Design group 120
Du Pont 9
dustbin lids 40
dye 56, 114, 124
Elastan 110
Elastex 110
elastic webbing 110
electrostatic sprayer 90
enamel paint 44, 63
epoxy 89, 120

Acknowledgments

The ProDesign series was developed from an original idea by Jean Koefoed.

The following people were very helpful in the preparation of this book. Its value, if any, is due to their generous assistance and also that of the manufacturers' representatives and designers whose works are discussed here.

Paola Antonelli, The Museum of
  Modern Art
Arlette Barré-Despond
Harriet Bee, The Museum of Modern Art
George M. Beylerian, Material Connexion
Dr. Claire Bonney
Judith Brauner, Vitra GmbH
Isabelle Denamur
Ann Dixon, The Museum of Modern Art
Olivier Gagnère
Alexander Gelman
Masaaki Gotsubo, Mazda Motor of
  America, Inc.
Arlene Hirst, *Metropolitan Home*
Gerard Laizé, V.I.A.
Ivan Luini, Luceplan USA Inc.
Tom Matano, Mazda Motor of America, Inc.
Murray Moss, Moss
Yuki Nishino, Mazda Motors Inc.
Susanne Papke, Vitra GmbH
Chee Pearlman, *I.D.*
Dianne H. Pilgrim, Cooper-Hewitt
  National Design Museum
Stephen Van Dyk, Cooper-Hewitt
  National Design Museum Library
Rémy Vreis, V.I.A.
Hideki Yamamoto

Permissions

Photography and artwork was generously provided by the following contributors, preceded by page numbers:

2 Matrix, divisione della Giorgetti S.p.A.
12-13 Richard A. McGrath, photographer
14-15 Matrix, divisione della Giorgetti S.p.A.
16-17 Quart de Poil'
19 Yellow Diva
20-21 Steinmann & Schmid
22-24 The Gehry Collection, courtesy of
  Knoll
26-27 Roberto Sellitto, photographer
28-29 Emilio Tremolada, photographer
30-31 Schnakenburg & Brahl,
  photographers
34-35 Vitra GmbH and Hans Hansen,
  photographer
36-37 Marino Ramazzotti, photographer
38-39 Carlo Forcolini
40-41 Diametrics
41-43 Vitra GmbH and Hans Hansen,
  photographer
44-47 King Size by Lasar
48-49 Andrés Otero
50-51 Vitra and Hans Hansen,
  photographer
52-53, 55 Eek en Ruijgrok vof
56-57 Sylvain Dubuisson
58-59 Matteograssi S.p.A.
60-62 Paolo Rizzatto and Cassina S.p.A.
64-66 Alberto Meda and Alias S.r.l.
68-71 Roberto Lucci
72-73 Frans Van Praet
74-75 Hans Hansen, photographer
77 Vitra GmbH
78-79 Kartell S.p.A.
80-81 Oscar Tusquets Blanca and Casas
82-83 Anna Castelli Ferrieri
84-85 Aaron Lown
86-89 MAP—Merchants of Australia
  Product Pty
90-91 Andrés Otero, photographer
92-93 Fabrizio Ballardini and Bernini
94-96 Pod
97 Pod (top), Maverick Recording
  Company (bottom)
98 Vitra GmbH
100 Hans Hansen, photographer
102-105 Alberto Meda
106 interpretation of an illustration by
  William Stumpf (middle), Herman Miller
  Inc. (bottom)
107-109 Herman Miller Inc.
110-111 Luciana Martins and Gerson de
  Oliveira
112-115 Vittorio Bonacina & C.
116-119 Pesce Ltd.

120 Marcel Wanders
121 Hans van der Mars
122 Sears, Roebuck & Co.
123 Constantin Boym
124-126 Andrés Otero, photographer
128 Alberto Liévore
129 Jordi Sarra, photographer
130 Aberto Liévore (top left and right),
  Rafael Vargas (bottom)
131 Alberto Liévore
132-133 Matteograssi S.p.A.
134-135 Quart de Poil'
136-137 Rimadesio
139-140 Fiam Italia S.p.A.
142-144 Fly Time S.r.l.
146-147 Quart de Poil'
1481-50 Witt Design
152-153, 155 Mazda Motor Corporation